Making Musical
Instruments

by Irving Sloane

CLASSIC GUITAR CONSTRUCTION
GUITAR REPAIR
STEEL-STRING GUITAR CONSTRUCTION
MAKING MUSICAL INSTRUMENTS

Irving Sloane

Making Musical Instruments

Illustrated with black-and-white photographs, drawings and full-color photographs.

A Sunrise Book
E. P. Dutton   New York

For information contact : E.P. Dutton, 2 Park Avenue,
New York, N.Y. 10016

Library of Congress Cataloging in Publication Data

Sloane, Irving.
Making musical instruments.

"A Sunrise book."
Bibliography: p.
1. Musical instruments—Construction. I. Title.
ML460.S64 781.9'1 77-26000

ISBN: 0-87690-293-X

Published simultaneously in Canada by Clarke, Irwin & Company
Limited, Toronto and Vancouver

Production by Stuart Horowitz

10 9 8 7 6 5 4 3 2 1

 First Edition

To Robert and Andrée Bouchet

CONTENTS

Introduction

In 1975 I moved from New York to Brussels and began working on the problems of building the instruments in this book. Through the extraordinary courtesy of René de Maeyer, director of the Brussels Museum of Musical Instruments, I was given a space to use as a workshop.

This book describes the construction of six instruments: two percussive (snare drum, tambourine), two plucked (banjo, dulcimer), one bowed (Hardanger fiddle), and one woodwind (alto recorder). With the exception of the recorder, these are basically folk instruments despite the sophisticated trappings of the snare drum and banjo. Along with presenting a representative cross-section of musical instruments, I have endeavored to explain most of the mechanical and decorative processes encountered in ordinary building practice.

The beginning section deals with the process of laminating veneers into hoops and shells for construction of the banjo, drum, and tambourine, all three of which are essentially frame drums employing skin heads. The dulcimer is the simplest plucked instrument to build, a good project for the beginner who may wish to move on to building guitars.

The Hardanger fiddle is a good introduction to the construction of fiddles and viols, a large and important area of instrument making. Several factors influenced my choice. Hardanger fiddles can be adapted by the maker to conform to individual levels of skill. They can be made as simply as many old fiddles were, or as complex as one's abilities will allow. There is no purfling, a tricky job for a novice,

and none of the perfection anxiety that goes with copying a Stradivarius. The Hardanger fiddle also has the advantage of encouraging artistic invention while providing all the fundamental techniques of violin making.

For the recorder, I sought the assistance of Arnold Dolmetsch Ltd., a pioneer firm in recorder construction, because I lacked the experience and equipment to make one. It is the most difficult project in this book because measurements are extremely critical and a subtle discrepancy can mean the difference between a good and a poor recorder. It is also an instrument where being a player as well as maker is a practical necessity.

Throughout, I have touched only superficially on the history of these instruments, a subject that has been expertly dealt with in other books. I have confined myself generally to observations that reflect my interest in the social history of musical instruments rather than their primitive origins.

My experience and training have been as a designer, a background that has focused my instrument building on the esthetics of musical instruments—their form, design, and surface enrichment. Although I have copied a few instruments for this book, I am happier designing my own style of drum or banjo. But always I follow, as closely as good sense and means permit, the principles of construction evolved by generations of instrument makers.

This book owes much to the edifying hours spent studying instruments in museum collections. Cultivating an appreciation for the beauty and surpassing craftsmanship of fine old instruments is an important part of instrument making. It is possible to copy some old instruments through blueprints available from museums but these tend to be research documents often lacking all the details necessary to build an exact replica. If you need to study a particular instrument, museums will usually cooperate if you first write to them about your requirements and manage to convey a reassuring level of seriousness. If you wish to bring your camera, check with the museum first. Some have restrictions about picture taking and a few charge hourly rates for photographing on their premises.

Two good books are available to craftsmen interested in reproducing instruments dating earlier than the eighteenth century: *Making Early Percussion Instruments* by Jeremy Montagu, and *The Amateur Wind Instrument Maker* by Trevor Robinson.

The building of musical instruments is more an art than a science, resting as it does on principles only imperfectly understood. Although much has been learned about the science of sound waves and acoustics, where instrument making is concerned it has served mainly to corroborate the empirical wisdom of ancient practice. No fundamental canons have been overturned and it is questionable whether the further unriddling of these mysteries will materially affect the work of instrument makers; they will be left with their instincts and judgments based on experience and intuition as were all the makers who preceded them. The construction of fine musical instruments will resist foolproof formulation, and the mystery that begins with a few pieces of wood and ends with the sound of a violin will remain to challenge talents and skills for which more satisfying employment could hardly be found.

Brussels 1977   *Irving Sloane*

Acknowledgments

Many individuals generously gave of their time to assist me in my researches. For their interest and advice I am indebted to Scott Odell (Smithsonian Institution); John O. Curtis (Sturbridge Village); Edouard-Aimé Jacobs (Belgian Royal Army Museum); John M. Frayler (First Corps of Cadets); Reidar Sevag (Norsk Folkemusikksamlung); Julia Raynsford (Victoria and Albert Museum). Valuable assistance with picture research was given by staff members of the National Army Museum in London.

For their thoughtful assistance, sincere thanks are due Michael Longworth, Scott E. Antes, Jeremy Montagu, Jacques Bayet, and good friend James F. Saporito. Gunter Amendt graciously supplied pictures of banjos in his collection and for their kind cooperation during my visit to Aldershot, I am grateful to Messrs Newell and Leech of Henry Potter & Company.

The recorder section came about through the unstinting collaboration of Dr. Carl Dolmetsch and his staff at the Arnold Dolmetsch Ltd. workshops in Haslemere, Surrey. I am particularly thankful to Kenneth Collins and Donald Clark, senior craftsmen of the recorder department for their patient help.

I am greatly indebted to René de Maeyer, director of the Brussels Museum of Musical Instruments, for his interest and support. Thanks also to those members of the museum staff who went out of their way in my behalf, namely Geert Vermeiren, Hubert Boone, Ann Caufriez, and Lode Bauwens.

Irving Sloane

Veneers, Glue, and Humidity

The laminating process essential to the construction of several of the instruments in this book makes considerable use of veneer. Hardwood veneers in a broad range of attractive grainings and hues are readily available to craftsmen needing only small quantities. I have so far used only unfigured maple veneer of standard thickness ($1/28''$) for the basic laminations, reserving exotic veneers for facings. Maple is relatively inexpensive, smooth grained, and can be had in large sheets running up to 16" x 8' or more. Birch or beech might work just as well, and the choice finally would hinge on price, sizes available, straightness of grain, and absence of open pores. Wide sheets simplify the cutting and assembly of cross-grain strips for cross-banding, and a smooth-grained surface makes finishing easier.

All the veneer laminating is done with clear epoxy, a two-part adhesive of exceptional strength. One part is the resin, and the other the hardener. The chief advantage of epoxy in gluing veneers is not its strength but the absence of water. Water-based glues distort thin veneers, making control of the gluing process a difficult, unpredictable business. Epoxy does not distort the wood, there is no shrinkage to contend with, and the slow setting time of epoxy makes a complex gluing operation a simple affair. At normal room temperature you always have about two hours of working time with a freshly mixed batch. Epoxy that has not hardened can be cleaned off tools with a rag moistened with acetone, and will wash off hands with soap and water.

The two-tube blister cards of epoxy sold in hardware stores are too expensive to use for laminating. The Devcon Corporation (Danvers, Mass.) markets a one-pound kit which sells for around six dollars. Under the trade names of Devco or Two-Ton it is available from industrial supply firms. A list of suppliers in your area can be obtained by writing to Devcon. A one-pound kit will easily suffice for making a drum, a banjo with resonator, and a tambourine.

In the building of musical instruments, epoxy should never be used on any part that may at some point have to be removed for repair, such as the plates of a violin or a fretboard. Violin plates should always be glued with animal or hide glue. Fretboards can be glued with hide glue or Titebond, an aliphatic resin glue available in most hardware stores. It is much stronger than polyvinyl resin emulsion glues (Elmer's Glue) and has a built-in tack for a fast initial grabbing action. Titebond dries to a hard film of creamy translucence resistant to lacquer and varnish solvents. It sands well and cures rapidly with a short clamping time.

Musical instruments in general, and stringed instruments in particular, should be built in a dry atmosphere. If you make a fiddle in an atmosphere containing about 65% relative humidity, it will probably crack if you move it to an area with a relative humidity level of 20%. Ideally, instruments should be built in a drier environment than the one in which they will most frequently be used. A good workshop level of relative humidity is about 45%. In the construction of those instruments which are essentially laminations, humidity is of negligible consequence.

Tools

The tools needed to make the instruments described here include both wood and metal working tools. Most of the woodworking tools are of the kind most craftsmen possess. A few specialized tools are important for certain aspects of instrument making and these appear as photographic footnotes in those chapters where they are used. My basic tool chest includes the following:

Saw
Hammer
Fine dovetail saw
Medium backsaw
Adjustable coping saw
$1/2''$, $1''$ gouges
$1/16''$, $1/4''$, $5/8''$ chisels
Files (flat, riffler, and needle)
Hand scrapers
Scraper blades with edge burnisher
Block plane
Wire nippers
Metal straightedge
Circle cutter
Assorted clamps
Utility knife
$3/8''$ power drill with drill stand
Dremel Moto-Tool with shaper base
Hand drill

Metalworking tools include:

Propane torch with fine and medium burner tips
Jeweler's saw
Parallel pliers
Chasing hammer
Nylon-faced hammer
Tongs
Tweezers
Tin snips
Hacksaw

All soldering is done with either soft or hard silver solder. Soft soldering is done with Brookstone Stay-Brite silver bearing solder, which is sold with a liquid flux (Brookstone catalog #1590.9). Hard soldering is done with Brookstone Safety-Silv silver solder (catalog #1592.5) with silver solder flux (catalog #1593.3). For Brookstone's address see Suppliers, page 159.

Cutting tools must be kept at razor sharpness for maximum working efficiency. Sharp tools are a pleasure to use and safer than dull ones. It is necessary to use more force with a dull tool, making a slip more likely, and a dull tool can cut you just as badly as a sharp one. A combination India stone (aluminum oxide) with medium- and fine-grit surfaces will do a good job of basic sharpening. For a surgical cutting edge a hard Arkansas stone is necessary.

Lubricate the stone with 3-in-One oil mixed with a little kerosene. The fluid floats away metal particles that might clog the stone. Hold the cutting bevel of the tool against the stone and hone with a small circular motion; it is easier to control an orbital motion than a long, sweeping motion that is likely to rock the bevel. When the bevel is as sharp as you can get it on the fine India stone, switch to the hard Arkansas stone. Hone until all scratches are gone, leaving the bevel shiny smooth. Turn the blade over and hold it flat against the stone. Remove the wire edge by moving the blade sideways about an inch. If the edge is properly sharpened, it will shave hair from the back of your hand. Repeat the fine honing until it does.

Gouges are sharpened with a sweeping, rolling motion as they are passed over the stone. The burr on the inner edge is removed with a wedge-shaped, round-nosed slipstone.

Scraper blades are a tool of basic importance to instrument makers. Their principal virtue is that they do not round edges the way sandpaper does, and they produce a fuzz-free, clean surface that cannot be duplicated with sandpaper. I use three rigid scraper blades of varying shape, and one curved scraper blade that is flexible.

Drawing an edge on a scraper blade is a job that requires some practice. The long edges must be honed dead flat and square by sliding the blade over the stone using a wooden support block to keep the blade perfectly vertical. The blade is then laid on its side and honed until the edge is knife-edge square. Position the blade on the edge of the workbench and draw a steel burnisher across the flat face of the blade along the edge. Do this once or twice to draw the edge, which you then turn over by holding the burnisher upright and running it across the edge at a slight angle. Oil the edge before burnishing.

For sanding I use two grades of garnet paper, #100(2/0) for coarse sanding, and #240(7/0) for fine sanding. Wet sanding of varnished surfaces is done with #400 and #600 wet-or-dry silicon carbide paper.

Laminate Shells and Hoops

The first three instruments in this book—the banjo, snare drum, and tambourine—all require the fabrication of a round wooden hoop or shell. In the past, the technical difficulties of making such hoops and shells have been formidable enough to keep amateur craftsmen from making these instruments.

Drum counter hoops, for example, have traditionally been made from a single piece of oak, ash, or beech steamed and strapped to a cylindrical form. The ends were glued together with a long scarf joint

2. Veneer and epoxy laminations

reinforced with clenched nails.

Bending wood with steam and drying it on a form requires special equipment—a trough or container for steaming and a cylindrical release form. Manipulating large steaming pieces of wood also requires practiced dexterity. It is easy to fracture the wood through hastily applied pressure or some hidden weakness in the wood. Hoops can also be formed on a heated bending iron but there are problems. It is extraordinarily difficult to bend wood of requisite thickness (5/16" minimum) into a relatively small circle. The wood must be presoaked in water and periodically dampened during a bending process which involves considerable physical effort. Moreover, cutting and joining the large scarf joint is a tricky affair requiring a circular form to ensure accuracy. Hoops of a larger diameter—18" up to bass drum size—can be bent more easily, with the steaming method to be preferred over the bending iron method. If you are bound to try, straight-grained beech is a wood with excellent bending properties.

Today, modern hardwood veneers and super-strong epoxy glue make it possible to build laminate hoops and shells of unequaled strength and stability. A simple, inexpensive release form supplies the pressure to glue veneers into a tight lamination with the dried epoxy films providing adhesion and structural rigidity.

3. *Nineteen ply banjo shell ready for removal from release form*

Release Form

Making a circular shell or hoop of laminated hardwood veneers requires a circular form that can generate pressure and then collapse radially so that the completed lamination can be removed. The laminations are confined by an outer retainer wall of spring steel banding (.015″) formed to the outside diameter of the shell or hoop.

If the retainer wall has an 11″ inside diameter and the release form has a 9½″ diameter, it will make a banjo shell of ¾″ thickness. But if the sum of the laminations adds up to a thickness of ¾″, no pressure, in fact, will result. Pressure is generated in one of two ways: by increasing slightly the diameter of the release form, or by increasing slightly the thickness of the lamination. A thin sheet of rubber is glued to the outer face of the release form sections so that pressure develops before the form reaches its full diameter. Alternatively, an additional strip of veneer can be inserted without glue to provide pressure.

The banjo release form consists of three pressed wood or plywood discs glued together to make a sandwich of not less than 2⅜″ thickness and 9½″ diameter. The circular discs are mounted on a fixed spindle 4¾″ from a bandsaw blade. They are then cut by revolving them against the saw blade. Discs can also be cut on a jigsaw, after which the glued-up sandwich is trued to a circle by revolving it against a sanding disc. Gluing is done with Titebond and clamping pressure. When dry, sand the exterior face smooth and check to make sure the form is a true circle. Draw a slightly larger circle on a white piece of cardboard and place the form within this circle to locate discrepancies. The release form cannot work efficiently if it is not a true circle.

Draw a line through the center of the form and another one bisecting the first at right angles. Drill four 3/4" holes, each hole centered on the bisecting lines 1 3/4" from the edge. Draw a line 1/8" from each side of the bisecting lines to serve as a guideline for sawing. Draw in the square center cutout. Saw out the bisecting 1/4" strips and the square cutout. This will free the four sections of the form, which must be numbered so they will always assemble in the same sequence.

Cut four pegs out of a 3/4" hardwood dowel. A 2" x 2" square hardwood center block can be made of glued-up stock. Taper slightly the bottom ends of the dowels and the square block to facilitate their entry into their holes. When the dowels and the square peg are in place, the form should have an outside diameter of 9 1/2". Finish the form by covering the outer curved face of each section with a thin sheet of rubber about 1/32" thick. Adhere with Plio-bond or other contact adhesive.

The retainer strip for the eleven-inch banjo shell requires two lengths of metal, one of which must be 34.55" (34 35/64") long. This strip forms the inner circle while the other strip serves as a glued reinforcement. The length of the strip is calculated

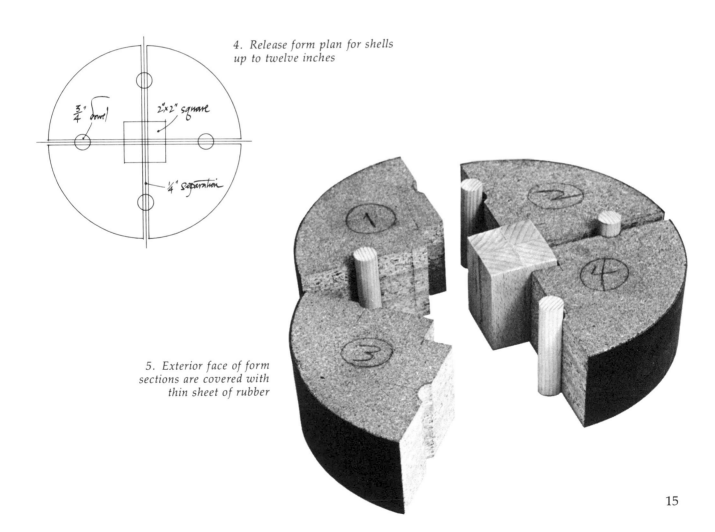

4. *Release form plan for shells up to twelve inches*

5. *Exterior face of form sections are covered with thin sheet of rubber*

15

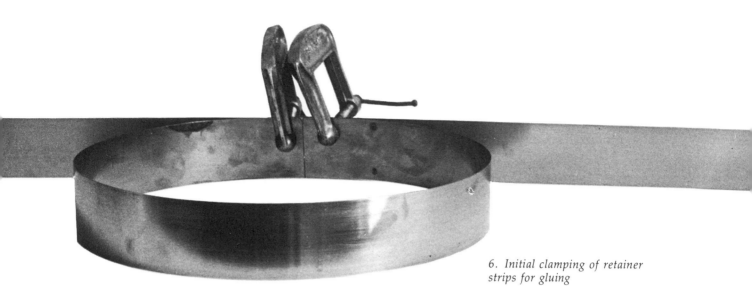

6. *Initial clamping of retainer strips for gluing*

by multiplying the diameter of 11″ by 3.141 (π). The width of the strips should be no less than 2⅜″, the thickness of the release form.

Clean both strips thoroughly with acetone and apply epoxy to one side of one of the strips. Clamp the end of the other strip to the middle of the glued strip and bend the accurately sized strip around in a circle until it butts against the clamped end. Clamp this end so that the joint remains firmly butted. The ends of the outer strip may not meet but that is unimportant. Use clothespins to keep the two strips under gluing pressure in a circle. The clothespins' clamping pressure can be brought up to Space Age standards by wrapping them with small rubber bands. Leave the glued retainer wall undisturbed for twenty-four hours. Remove the clothespins and wrap glass filament tape around the form. Avoid squeezing or distorting the retainer wall, which might crack the glue joint. The shear strength of epoxy is great, but its peel strength is poor on metal.

This same kind of release form and retainer wall setup is used to make the tambourine shells and the drum hoops. For shells or hoops that are fairly close in diameter, the same form can sometimes be employed through the use of unglued filler strips. When making laminate shells with a diameter larger than 12″, such as the drum hoops and banjo resonator, provision should be made for two round pegs along each quadrant.

7. *Retainer strip glued and clamped*

16

Lamination Procedure

Maple or birch veneer of standard $1/28''$ thickness is readily available in large sheets, and the wider the sheet, the less work there is in preparing the lamination. I prefer maple because it is harder and smoother than birch.

Continuing with the 11" banjo shell, it is a lamination made of twenty-three veneer strips. This number will make a shell of approximately $3/4''$ thickness. A $5/8''$ shell will take nineteen strips. These thicknesses are not critical and will vary depending on the exact thickness of the veneer.

The twenty-three veneer strips are divided into twelve long-grain strips and eleven cross-grain strips. The strips are first cut to size and eleven long-grain strips are glued to eleven cross-grain strips to make eleven double strips. These eleven cross-banded strips plus one single long-grain strip comprise the basic lamination. All laminations are an odd number of strips so that the finishing inside strip is always a long-grain strip.

Cut off a 35" section from your veneer sheet. Use a knife such as a Stanley utility knife with blades inside the handle. Cut the long-grain strips with a metal straightedge as a guide. Cut slowly and carefully with several light incisions rather than one powerful slice because the grain may throw the knife off course. Banjo shells are $2^3/8''$ in depth and the lamination strips should be cut $1/16''$ wider to allow for some trim during finishing. Cut the cross-grain strips with two strokes and then snap them back and off. Cut their ends square and butt them with a small strip of plastic tape to hold them together. Cut enough to cover the length of each of the long-grain strips.

Mix together an equal quantity of epoxy resin and hardener until they make a uniformly colored mix. Apply the glue to a long-grain strip using a scrap of veneer as a spatula. Cover the surface with a light but not skimpy coat of epoxy, making sure that no spot is left bare. Press a taped cross-grain strip against the glue-covered surface of the long-grain strip. Wrap a piece of tape around the two

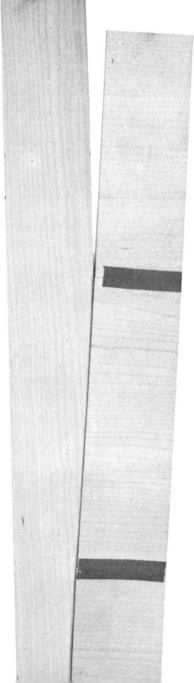

8. Long-grain and cross-grain maple veneer strips

strips in about six places to ensure that the strips will stay in alignment while under pressure. Place this double strip along the edge of a sheet of freezer wrap or waxed paper. Roll it over so that both sides are covered by paper, and as each double strip is assembled, roll it up in the wrap. When you have wrapped five or six double strips, make a tight bundle of it by again wrapping some tape around the bundle to keep the pieces in alignment. Place this bundle between two 1″ x 3″ x 36″ boards and clamp every six inches. It is best to glue no more than six double strips at one time. Two separate bundles have to be prepared to get the eleven double strips needed for the shell.

Leave the bundles under pressure overnight and then remove the wrapping and all tapes. Clean off traces of the tape adhesive with a cloth moistened with acetone or naphtha. Scrape off any dried glue on the flat surfaces of the strips and run a small block plane or file over the edges to remove any globules of glue ooze. The strips are now ready to be fitted into the form in a preliminary lay-up using no glue.

Lay in the first strip with the long-grain side against the retainer wall. Press it against the wall

9. *Bundle of glued double strips under pressure*

using clamps if necessary to ensure a tight fit. Mark the juncture and saw off the ends square so that the strip snaps into place when it is put back in the form. Number each strip to preserve their sequence and spot the end joints so that they fall in different places. It is impossible to produce a lamination with all ends butted. Under pressure they will separate and plugs sawed off the cutoff ends must be inserted to fill the holes after the shell is laminated. After eleven double strips have been laid in, put in the single long-grain strip.

Position the four sections of the release form and insert the pegs beginning with the square center peg. Use a hammer to drive in the pegs and check the openings between the sections to see that they are uniformly spaced. If not, small wedges will have to be inserted to wedge the sections into parallel adjustment so that the form will assume the circular shape it must have to exert even pressure. If pressure is being applied unequally, it is because the release form is out of round. To check the accuracy of the form's circle, draw a circle slightly larger than the form on a white cardboard. Place the form in the center of the circle to check its outer concentricity. Deviations are seldom more than minor and can be corrected by strategic wedging.

If, after all the pegs are in place, no pressure results, an additional filler strip must be added to the lamination. This filler can be another strip of veneer or a strip of steel banding or thin plastic, depending on how much filler is needed to generate pressure. Problems of this sort are to be expected and point up the obvious necessity, in the case of the snare drum, of making the hoops before the drum shell. The drum shell can easily be formed to match the hoops; no adjustment is possible in the hoops once they are made.

Make a final test of the form under pressure after a filler is inserted. The pegs should require solid hammer blows to wedge the form out with adequate gluing pressure. The square center peg may fall out when the pegs are driven in but that will not affect gluing pressure. It can be wedged back in with strips of veneer for an extra ounce of pressure if needed. Enough pressure must be generated to

10. *Applying epoxy to double strip*

11. *Fitting strips into form*

press the veneers into gap-free contact all around the form. When this has been achieved, remove the form and all the strips except the first one. Apply epoxy to the long-grain surface of the second strip and press it into place. Glue in all the strips and replace the release form plus any filler strips you have added. Drive home the pegs and use the wedges to wedge the form into concentricity with the circle on the cardboard. If an excess of glue ooze appears, wipe it off with a damp cloth. Leave undisturbed overnight.

Lamination will go smoothly if these additional cautions are observed:

1. The height or thickness of the release form and retainer wall must be at least as great as the lamination. If the height of the retainer wall and form are greater than the lamination, it should be centered on the form before pressure is applied. Begin the lay-up by laying in each strip against the base of the form, tapping them into alignment with a small block of wood as you go along. After the lay-up is completed, tap the whole lamination up to a central position in the form.

2. Gluing of the lamination to the retainer wall and release form can be avoided by spraying the inside face of the retainer wall and the rubber covering of the release form with silicone spray.

Finally, it is important to understand that if your shell or hoop turns out slightly out of round, it will still work fine. A true round is perhaps of most importance for a banjo shell that is going to have a resonator and flange. But even here, absolute roundness is not crucial; a flat spot can be positioned at the neck joint. Fortunately, the thick lamination of a banjo shell makes a circle easier to control than on the larger diameter, thinner hoops where perfect roundness is less critical.

After the lamination has dried, knock out the pegs and remove the release form. Lift and slam the form down on the workbench to shock loose the lamination. Use a small block of wood and a hammer, tapping around the edge of the lamination to gradually work it down and free of the retainer wall.

Clamp two boards to the workbench, forming a

19

12. *Hammering in dowels generates pressure*

13. *Knocking out finished shell*

14. *Raw laminate banjo shell*

15. *Small wedges are used to align sections*

corner where the rough shell can be immobilized while the top and bottom edges are smoothed. Use a block plane, rasp, and hand scraper to true the edges. Keep the shell rotating in a constant, regular motion to ensure uniform removal of wood. Smooth both edges true and square.

Fill the holes left by the separated ends with epoxy and plug them with small plugs cut from the waste pieces of the double strips. Taper the plugs slightly and drive them in with a small hammer. If you intend to leave the edges exposed (unveneered), the holes should be filled with care, the veneers aligned to make an unbroken appearance in the strip.

Fill gaps in the face of the shell by first giving them a slight taper. If you have saved all the cutoff ends of the double strips, you can probably find the original piece that will make a perfect match for the gap. Saw off a slightly oversize tapered filler piece. Fit it by slowly filing and testing it until it is almost wedged all the way. Apply epoxy, drive the filler strip in flush with the edges, and clamp with a wooden caul and protective piece of waxed paper. When the patch dries, sand it level with the surrounding surface.

Making a twenty-three-ply lamination sounds like more work than it really is. It takes me less than five hours of working time from the cutting of the strips until the shell is under pressure. The reward is a banjo shell incomparably stronger and more stable than any you can buy.

Exotic Face Veneers

Laminate shells can be faced with attractive hardwood veneers such as rosewood, curly maple, walnut, satinwood, macassar ebony, and many others. The standard thickness for veneers is $1/28''$ but many today are cut to $1/30''$ and $1/40''$. Thinly cut veneers will work as a facing if no inlay is planned. Inlay work inevitably involves a good deal of surface sanding and $1/40''$ is playing it close.

In all cases where a decorative face veneer is used, it should first be glued to a long-grain backing strip unless it is a full $1/28''$. Veneer of this thickness can be treated as the first strip in a lamination and should be glued to a cross-grain backing. The same is true for both exterior and interior facings. Veneer facings present no laminating problems unless you are using a burl veneer. Burls, when you buy them, present an uneven, waffled surface and before they can be used, must be made perfectly flat.

Cut the burl into strips with a large margin for trim ($2^3/4''$ wide for a $2^3/8''$ banjo shell). Cut the strips to display the most attractive figure, free of blemishes. Do not worry about pinholes, a common feature of burl veneers. After all the strips are cut, moisten some paper toweling and interleave it between the veneer strips. Use at least two sheets between each strip and clamp the pile between two boards. Apply slight clamping pressure at first to avoid cracking the veneer. As the veneer absorbs moisture from the toweling, pressure can be gradually increased. After full pressure is achieved, leave under pressure for two hours.

Remove the clamps and discard the toweling. Interleave dry paper towels between the veneer strips, which should be flat by now. Apply pressure and change the towels for some dry toweling in two hours. Leave under pressure until ready to glue. When ready, remove from the press and cut the ends of the strips square. Butt the strips together to find the arrangement that gives the best flow of pattern. If you give the strips a quick wash coat of shellac (1 part shellac, 5 parts alcohol), it makes matching easier. Slice the butt joints with a single-edge razor so that they make the tightest possible joint and tape them together with one-inch plastic tape. Apply epoxy to a long-grain maple veneer strip cut to the same size as the burl facing. Press the burl against the glued surface and tape the two veneers together in about five places to prevent shifting under pressure. Wrap in freezer wrap and clamp between two boards.

Before gluing burls make sure that they are completely dry. Also more care is necessary when inlaying burl facings; they tend to fragment around mortise edges. Pinholes and other defects can be filled with a filler of epoxy mixed with a powdered pigment of the appropriate color.

16. *Applying epoxy to Carpathian elm burl strip*

Banjo

17. *Left to right:*
   Six-string banjo with dyed wood inlays, English c. 1850
   Seven-string banjo, English c. 1880–1885
   Six-string "piccolo" banjo, c. 1880–1885, Bacon, London
   (Gunter Amendt Collection)

No instrument mirrors the American spirit more invincibly than the banjo. Since the dawn of the republic, its bright stridency has enlivened the American musical scene and earned it recognition as the most nearly indigenous American instrument.

Presumably, African slaves brought to America the banjo or "banjar" as Thomas Jefferson called it in his *Notes on the State of Virginia* (1785). Evidence to back this theory is circumstantial and leaves unexplained why the banjo did not also take root in the West Indies and South America, areas with large populations of African slaves.

Stringed instruments with a skin stretched over a hollow resonating chamber are an ancient invention known to many cultures besides African. Their use predates the Christian era by at least two thousand years, and they were widely known throughout Asia Minor and the Far East.

An American banjo player named Joel Walker Sweeney is believed to have introduced, in 1831, the fifth string, a high-pitched drone string that gives the five-string banjo its characteristic ring. Interest in the banjo grew with the rise of the blackface minstrel show. Sweeney himself was a famous minstrel and public enthusiasm for this form of vaudeville continued through the last half of the nineteenth century.

The banjo's popularity as a show business instrument brought some technical innovations. Novel metal tone rings and a resonator were added to make the sound brassier and louder, and the instrument itself became an increasingly gaudy extension of the performer. Mother-of-pearl and abalone inlay plus chrome- and gold-plated fitments accentuated the show business orientation of the banjo and reached their opulent zenith with the Paramount and Bacon & Day banjos of the early 1930's.

Banjos are relatively simple to make because all of the basic parts and hardware can be bought from companies like Stewart-MacDonald (Suppliers, page 159). But if you build the major parts—the shell, neck, flange, and resonator—yourself, you can have a fine, individually styled banjo for much less money than a good commercial banjo.

18. *Five-string banjo, tacked vellum,*
English c. 1840 (Victoria and Albert Museum)

Shell

Banjo shells differ according to playing style. Old-time players like an open-back banjo with rim thickness of $^1/_2"$ to $^5/_8"$, a head between $10^1/_2"$ and $10^3/_4"$, and a relatively subdued tone. Bluegrass players prefer resonator banjos with $^3/_4"$ shell, eleven-inch head, and machined tone rings. Bluegrass banjos are heavy and meant to be loud. Shell depth is normally $2^3/_8"$ but can be changed to suit individual preference. If you do change this depth, all measurements given here for a $2^3/_8"$ depth will have to be revised to work for your depth and hardware. Older banjos employed a hardwood dowel for reinforcing thin rims, and resonator banjos use a rim rod with screw coupler to adjust neck pitch. In my banjos I use no interior supports or rods because of the exceptional rigidity of laminate shells and because the neck is carefully pitched at the outset.

Make or purchase a banjo shell 11" in outside diameter and $2^3/_8"$ in height. The cost of materials

19. *Twenty-three ply burl faced shell uses about 16 sq. ft. of veneer*

20. *Leveling top and bottom of shell*

21. Burl shell with ball lugs, bracket hooks, tension hoop, and skin head

for a laminate shell is roughly one-fifth the cost of a commercially available raw, unfaced shell. It is not really worthwhile, however, to make your own plated tension hoop.

For the interior face of the open-back banjo shell I used curly maple; the exterior face and bottom of the shell are veneered with Carpathian elm burl. Flattened strips of the burl veneer were butted and taped together in a circle. They were then glued to a backing of maple veneer and the circle was cut out to the full ¾" width of the shell. It was glued to the bottom edge of the shell with epoxy and trimmed flush. The edges were cut away by hand with a purfling cutter to permit installation of an ivoroid corner strip edged on top and side by black-white wood purfling strips. This purfling was made up of two separate strips with grain oriented to

bend around the circle. The strips were glued in simultaneously with the ivoroid strip and taped down until dry. Duco cement was used and the plastic tape was wrapped completely around the shell wall to hold the binding strips.

The Sho-boat banjo shell has a ⅝" wall thickness and a facing of Brazilian rosewood with the grain running vertically. A corner ledge was cut out of the bottom outside corner and bound with a separating strip of black-white purfling and a strip of brass. The twenty-two gauge brass strip was cut to exact size and hard-soldered into a ring sized for a force fit. After the black-white strips were glued in with Titebond, epoxy was applied to the ledge and the brass ring hammered on.

Both shells were filled and finished with clear polyurethane varnish in the same way as the reso-

22. Nineteen ply rosewood faced shell with bracket shoes installed

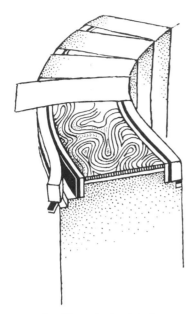

23. *Plan of edge binding on bottom edge of burl shell*

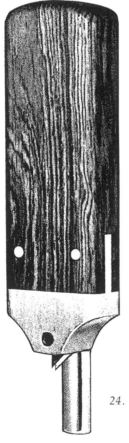

24. *Adjustable purfling cutter (Ibex)*

nator. (See page 40.)

If you are using a notched tension hoop, drop it down around the shell. Situate the back of the hoop with the cutout for string clearance next to the least attractive spot on the shell. With the hoop resting on the table and equidistant from the shell at all points, mark the positions for all twenty-four bracket holes. Lay a strip of paper on the shell and mark off the space between two bracket markings. Move the strip around the shell to check the accuracy of the spacing. Unless the holes are drilled at correctly spaced intervals, the hooks will engage the tension hoop notches at an angle instead of vertically. Drill all the bracket holes one inch on center from the bottom of the shell.

If you are using a grooved tension hoop with flat hooks, draw a line down the shell where you want the back and front to fall. Set a pair of dividers to $1^{5}/_{32}''$ and strike off this distance each side of the back line. Strike off a distance of $^{29}/_{32}''$ each side of your front line. These lines represent the first and last bracket holes on each side of the shell. Divide this distance by eleven to find the spacing for the other ten holes on each side. Take all surface measurements with a strip of paper pressed against the curved shell and then measure it flat.

Before drilling the front center hole for the bracket that will hold the tailpiece bolt, check your tailpiece to make sure the bolt is long enough to work from the bracket position. Drill two holes in the back center line for the neck lag bolts. Drill the lower hole $^{3}/_{4}''$ from the bottom edge and another hole $^{7}/_{8}''$ above it.

All drill holes in the shell should be sized so that the bolts will push through without screwing. A round wooden caul clamped inside the shell will prevent fracture of the interior face when the drill exits.

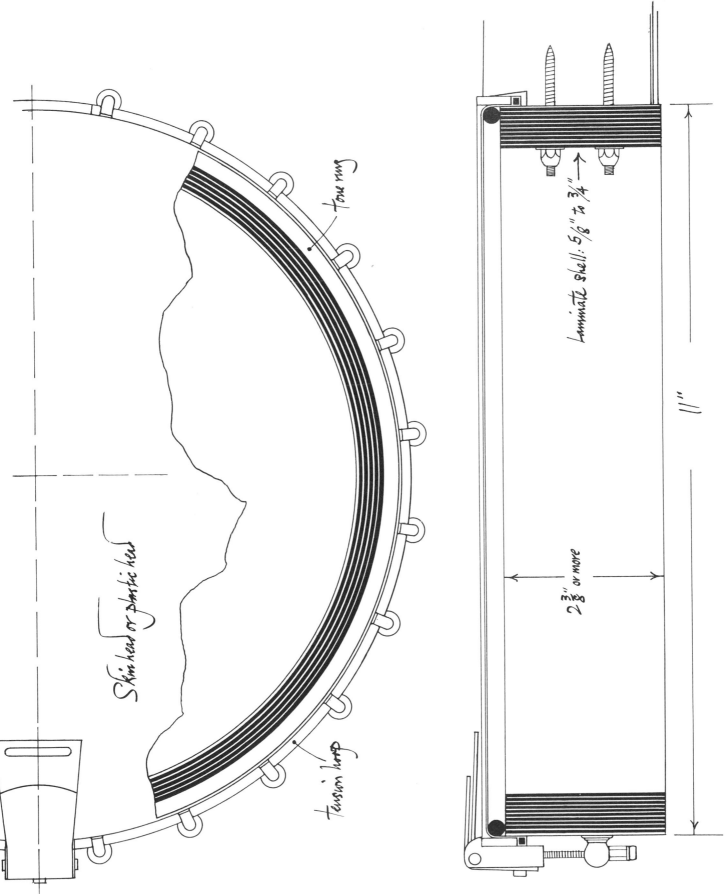

Skin head or plastic head

tone ring

tension hoop

Laminate shell: 5/8" to 3/4"

11"

2 1/8" or more

25. Basic banjo shell plan

Tone Rings and Heads

The simplest form of tone ring is a ¼″ brass rod soldered into a ring with the same outside diameter as the shell being used. Start with a rod at least four feet long; it is difficult to bend the ends unless there is space for a hand grip. Bend the rod into a hoop and braze or hard-solder the ends in a neat butt joint. Hammering the ring with a slightly domed hammer will make it round and replace the hardness lost in the heat of soldering. Polish the ring with emery cloth until shiny smooth. It can be left as is or nickel plated.

An interesting variation is a ring made of stainless steel or nickel-silver tubing with ⅛″ holes drilled at 1½″ intervals on the inner face. Tubing is best bent by starting with a very long piece, fastening one end to a correctly sized drum, and wrapping the tubing around the drum in one continuous motion. This kind of tone ring will produce a somewhat louder sound than a solid ring.

On my banjos I use calfskin heads, which I tuck myself. Premounted skin heads are sold but you can save about half the cost if you do it yourself. A top-quality fourteen-inch calfskin head from H. Band & Company (Suppliers, page 159) sells for under eight dollars (1977 prices).

I began by hard-soldering a ⅛″ x ½″ brass strip into a circle with an outside diameter of 11⁵⁄₁₆″. From this hoop I hacksawed two rings which came down to a height of ⁵⁄₃₂″ after being filed smooth. Each ring was hammered on its inside face to make it a true circle and to harden it. All edges were slightly rounded to avoid cutting the skins.

The skins—one a top-grade white calf, the other a cloudy-calf grade—were each 14″ in diameter. Unlike wooden flesh hoops, metal flesh hoops require an additional tuck to hold the skins securely because the skins' natural gluing propensity does not work on metal. Soak and lap as described in Drum Heads and Lapping, page 62. A lapping tool with a shorter right-angle bend is necessary for managing the extra tuck. Use a small saucer under the center of the skin to handle the slack while lapping. Clamp clothespins to the top and bottom face of the lapped sections to hold them until set. After the lapped edge has set—thirty minutes or so—remove the clothespins and set the head in place on the tone ring and shell, affix tension hoop and hooks, and screw down the tension hoop until the flesh hoop engages the shell. Leave to dry at least ten hours before screwing down to playing tension.

Calfskin heads have a mellow, less crisp tone than Mylar heads and are affected by humidity. The need for frequent adjustment makes them more suitable for an open-back banjo than a resonator banjo because the tension can be more easily regulated. A simple tone ring such as employed here calls for a medium- or high-crown plastic head.

26. Hard-soldering brass tone ring joint

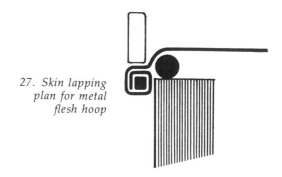

27. Skin lapping plan for metal flesh hoop

Neck

Banjo necks are independent extensions bolted to the shell. Since they carry all the frets—normally twenty-two for a five-string banjo—they are long compared to a guitar where a good portion of the fretboard rests on the body. This attenuated length plus the pressure exerted by steel strings makes a banjo neck particularly susceptible to warp unless it is reinforced. Bowing, a curvature of the neck characterized by a widening of the gap between strings and frets, is the major problem, and several methods are employed to combat this hazard.

Most commercial banjos have an adjustable truss rod let into a curved channel in the neck. The steel rod is anchored at the heel end of the neck, passes under a curved wood insert in the central portion of the neck, and ends in an exposed threaded terminus in the head. A hex nut working against a face-plate draws the rod up tight against the insert, thus exerting upward pressure on the central portion of the neck (30). Adjustable truss rods are designed to correct only a moderate degree of neck bow; they cannot cure a twisted neck or one with back-bow. Banjo necks are also reinforced with metal bars simply channeled into the neck.

Adjustable truss rods have their drawbacks. In their cheapest form, they are thin rods let into an oversize channel routed the length of the neck, considerably weakening the neck and inviting the problem the rod is designed to cure. Moreover, many banjo and guitar necks are damaged by their owner's inopportune or improper adjustment of truss rods. Putting a lot of tension on a truss rod during a dry spell will twist a neck during a subsequent period of high humidity. Rods also break under excessive tightening, producing an internal rattle unless replaced. A steel bar fitted into a channel in the neck, in my view, is a more attractive solution than an adjustable truss rod, but has the disadvantage of adding substantially to the weight of an already heavy instrument.

In my banjo necks I use a vertebrate truss rod, a variation of a reinforcement I devised for steel-string

28. *Five string banjo with burl faced peg head and shell, cloudy-calf head*

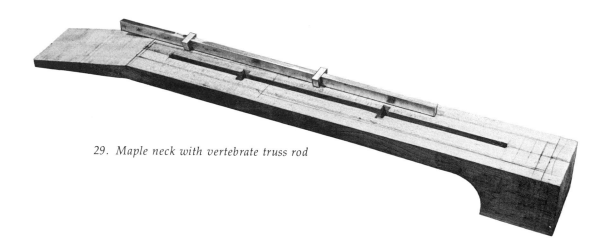

29. *Maple neck with vertebrate truss rod*

guitars. It consists of a central bar of $5/16''$ x $1/2''$ x $17''$ #2024 aluminum with two transverse pieces affixed to the bar. This assembly is let into a channel exactly sized to accommodate it. The #2024 aluminum is a heat-hardened aluminum used in the aviation industry and is not to be confused with the aluminum bar stock commonly sold in hardware stores.

The bar and transverse pieces are mortised to fit together in eggcrate fashion. All the mortises are slightly tapered so they can be hammered together to make a rigidly wedged joint without soldering or brazing. The reinforcing principle is based on the idea that it is much more difficult to bend a six-inch metal bar than one seventeen inches long. Breaking up the long bar with the transverse pieces considerably enlarges the amount of stress required to bow the center section. The truss assembly is glued in place with epoxy and for maximum effectiveness the mortise should be a gentle force fit. If a hammer is

required to drive in the truss, you risk splitting the neck.

The Sho-boat neck was made from a maple block 4″ x 2¹/₂″ x 24″. Because the wood was cut 45 degrees off the quarter, I sawed it in half lengthwise and tumbled one half end over end to strengthen the neck. While it was in two pieces I routed half the width of the truss channel in each piece and cut the inclined mortises for the transverse pieces. Both halves were then glued together with epoxy and clamped overnight.

The side profile of the neck was drawn on the side of the block and cut out on a bandsaw. I prefer to cut the long vertical shape of the neck with a hand saw because the saw can be angled for a good head start on the final shaping of the heel and the underside of the neck. The head contour was not cut out until the veneer sandwich facing was glued on.

Rough shaping of the heel was done with gouge and rasp. The largest chunks were cut away

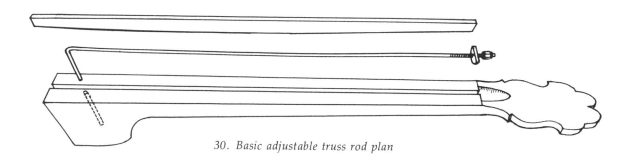

30. *Basic adjustable truss rod plan*

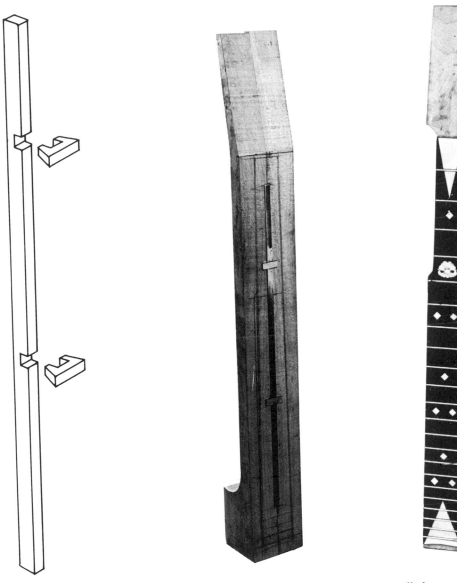

31. *Vertebrate truss rod*

32. *Neck with rod installed and with fretboard glued on*

with a 1″ gouge struck with a hammer. Rasp and curved scraper blade defined the shape for final smoothing with garnet paper.

The long shape of the neck was formed with a spokeshave and concave scraper blade. The rasp was used for truing the shape, and final finish was obtained with scraper and sandpaper.

A sandwich of $^3/_{32}″$ ebony, maple, and rose-wood veneer was glued together to make the Sho-boat head facing but was not mounted until all inlay was completed. The open-back banjo has a facing of Carpathian elm veneer glued to two layers of maple veneer and a final layer of black-dyed veneer.

The heel cap on both banjos is a sandwich of $^3/_{32}″$ ebony, maple, and black-dyed veneer to continue the side line motif carried on the head.

31

*33. Plan of banjo neck construction
and full-size plan of head*

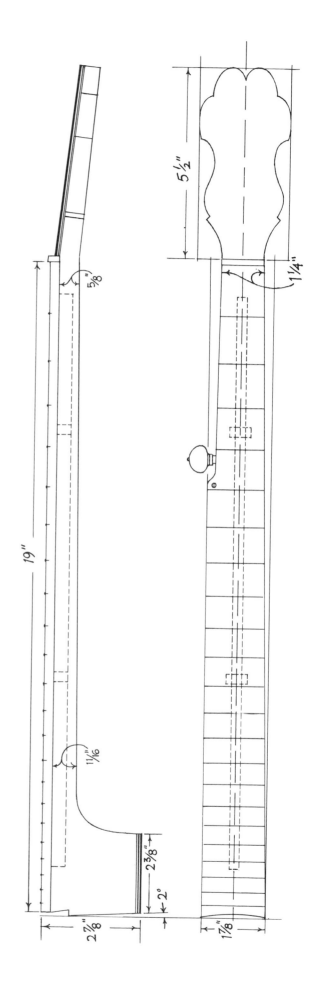

26¹/₄" FRET SCALE
(667 mm open string length)

Fret	Nut to fret inches	Nut to fret millimeters
1.	1.4718	37.384
2.	2.8611	72.672
3.	4.1725	105.982
4.	5.4104	137.424
5.	6.5789	167.104
6.	7.6818	195.118
7.	8.7229	221.562
8.	9.7056	246.522
9.	10.6332	270.083
10.	11.5088	292.324
11.	12.3353	313.766
12.	13.1155	333.134
13.	13.8519	351.838
14.	14.5471	369.496
15.	15.2033	386.164
16.	15.8227	401.897
17.	16.4074	416.748
18.	16.9593	430.766
19.	17.4802	443.997
20.	17.9719	456.486
21.	18.4360	468.274
22.	18.8741	479.402

27" FRET SCALE
(685.8 mm open string length)

Fret	Nut to fret inches	Nut to fret millimeters
1.	1.5147	38.475
2.	2.9457	74.763
3.	4.2957	109.053
4.	5.5701	141.399
5.	6.7716	171.936
6.	7.9083	200.745
7.	8.9802	227.961
8.	9.9900	253.611
9.	10.9458	277.830
10.	11.8476	300.726
11.	12.6981	322.326
12.	13.500	342.684
13.	14.2587	361.962
14.	14.9742	380.133
15.	15.6492	392.958
16.	16.2864	413.478
17.	16.8858	428.760
18.	17.4474	443.151
19.	17.9901	456.732
20.	18.4950	469.557
21.	18.9729	481.707
22.	19.4238	493.155

34. Rounding neck with spokeshave

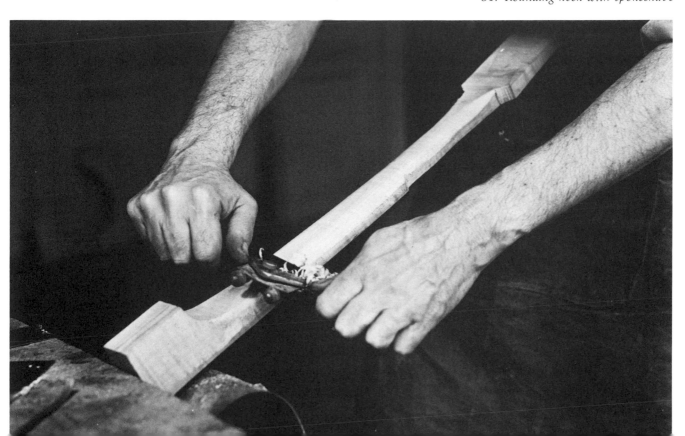

36. Ibex Fret Rule

35. Basic fretting tools

Fretboard

Drill a small hole in each corner of the fretboard, outside the actual shape of the fretboard. Fasten it to a larger workboard with a small brad in each hole. Sink the brads well below the surface with a nail set.

Smooth this side of the fretboard dead level with scraper blade and long sanding block. When a metal straightedge shows that the surface is level, remove the brads and turn the board over. Replace the brads, sinking them below the surface.

Traditionally, fret posiions have been laid out to a formula known as the rule of the eighteenth. The vibrating string length is divided by 18 to locate the first fret. The remaining string length is again divided by 18 to find the second fret and so on. This formula contains a slight error because 18 is an approximate figure. The precise figure is 17.835, and the scales listed here have been computed with this divisor.

Several scales are used in banjo making, the modern standard for five-string banjo being 26¼". Bluegrass players prefer a scale this long or longer, where tunings are usually C or G. Clawhammer-style players like a shorter scale—around 25"—so they can tune to A or D without a capo. Two scales are listed here, 26¼" and 27". On my banjos I took a 26⅛" scale from a fret rule available from most suppliers of instrument-making materials. This accurately etched rule (Ibex Fret Rule) also lists scales of 25²¹/₃₂", 25¹¹/₃₂", and 24²⁷/₃₂".

Before laying out the frets, draw the fretboard pattern on the board, making sure it is centered and that one side of the board is exactly parallel to the center line of the fretboard drawing. Mark the fret slots with a pointed metal scriber, working against the blade of a try square held against the parallel side. Start the slots with a dovetail saw or small backsaw, also working against the try square.

Fretting will go smoothly if the slot is correctly sized to the fret wire. I use a medium size (.078") nickel silver fret wire and a matching saw that will make a .023" slot in ebony. Fretting a rosewood board, a softer wood, requires a narrower slot, .020″.

Make sure that your slot matches the studded tang of the wire you are using by sawing a trial slot in a waste portion of your fretboard. Hammer in the test wire with an overhang of ⅛″ on each end. It should go in with a few taps and stay there. Crimp over the overhang with a light tap; if the fret is loose, it will rise in the middle. If the slot is too narrow, inordinate force will be required to anchor the fret, a dangerous practice because the accumulated wedging action of such fretting will bend a neck over backward. Wedge-fretting, in fact, is a standard repair technique for correcting a bowed neck.

There are three remedies for a loose slot; using a thinner saw, hammering or slightly filing off the set of your saw's teeth to make it thinner, or switching to a heavier gauge fret wire. But take the time to achieve an effective mating of fret wire to slot.

After sawing a few strokes in all the slots, cut out the shape of the fretboard. If you plan any inlay on the fretboard face, do it now. (See page 46.) And if you plan to bind the edges of the fretboard with plastic, the ledges must be routed now. I rout the ledges with a Dremel Moto-Tool using an adjustable base attachment and their #115 cutter. Check the cut on a scrap before routing the fretboard. The curved portion around the fifth fret cannot be routed but must be chiseled by hand.

Draw the exact fretboard shape on the top face of the neck and glue on the fretboard with Titebond. Lightly coat the gluing areas on the fretboard and neck and clamp with five or six clamps over a long board. This board should be preferably of hardwood and sized to cover the fretboard. Apply clamps with wood cauls under the neck to protect the surface. Watch the fretboard for any sign of shifting while applying clamping pressure. Increase clamping pressure slowly until you are sure the glue tack has set up to where it will hold, and then screw the clamps tight. Titebond has a fast tack and this whole clamping process takes only a few minutes. Clean off glue ooze with a damp cloth and keep under pressure overnight.

Remove the clamps and cauls and saw in all the

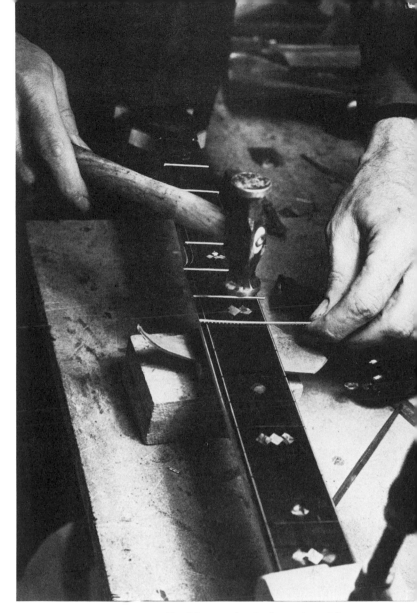

37. Hammering in fret wire with support under neck

frets to a full ¹/₁₆″ depth. Dress the entrance of each slot with a three-cornered file to chamfer each edge slightly. This will facilitate future fret removal, if necessary, without chipping the face of the fretboard.

Cut all the frets beforehand, allowing for a ⅛″ overhang on each end. Drop one or two drops of water into each fret slot with an eyedropper as fretting proceeds. Position each fret wire and drive it in with the polished, slightly domed face of any medium-weight hammer. If there are any scars on the hammer face they will transfer to the fret wire. A few good taps should seat a fret. Use a support

35

under the neck where you are hammering.

Cut off all the ends with a flush-cutting nipper and file them flush using a ten-inch flat-mill smooth file. When the ends are all flush, file a bevel on the bead ending of each fret. Always file frets in a manner that tends to push them into the slot rather than pull them out. Apply strips of ¼" masking tape alongside each fret to protect the fretboard while you are filing frets.

Gently glide a long carborundum stone or flat file over the tops of the frets. This will level out any unevenness and leave a flat ridge along the tops of some frets. Each fret must be filed and rounded until this flat ridge disappears. The fret ends are rounded off with a #2 extrafine pillar file. This file is immensely more useful if the edges are ground off with a belt sander so that they are shiny smooth and slightly rounded. Finish off the frets with a worn piece of crocus cloth. If you are not using any binding on the fretboard, fill side gaps under the fret ends with lampblack and epoxy filler for an ebony fretboard, burnt umber and epoxy for rosewood.

Binding strips can be installed with Duco ce-ment but I prefer to use a glue made of the plastic dissolved in acetone. Ivoroid and most plastic bindings will readily dissolve in acetone. Small bits of the plastic binding are snipped off and placed in a clear bottle with enough acetone to cover. Stopper and leave to dissolve. Shake it up occasionally and add acetone if it looks too thick. When completely dissolved and the consistency of white glue, tilt the neck and leak a bead of glue into the corner of the binding ledge along its entire length. Immediately press the binding strip in place. If any portion does not adhere, work some glue into the joint and press for ten seconds.

Jet-black ebony is impossible to find; streaks or veinings of gray are common. If unobtrusive, they will eventually disappear, darkened by the oil and perspiration of the player's hand. They can be removed by staining with any good black leather dye. Finish the fretboard with a light coat of refined linseed oil polished to a soft sheen with a clean rag.

Position markers can be made in white plastic binding by making holes with a fine drill or sharp awl and filling with lampblack and epoxy filler.

38. *Nested abalone and pearl squares, double line edge binding*

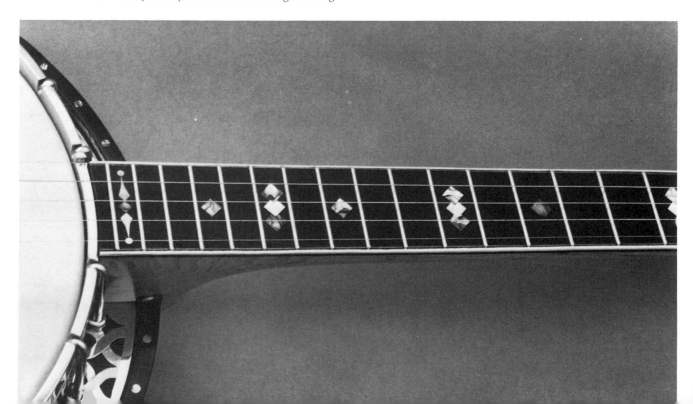

Resonator

Prepare a laminate hoop 13⁵/₈″ outside diameter x 1⁵/₈″ deep. An eleven-ply lamination will give you a wall thickness of appximately ³/₈″. Cut the laminate strips to full 1⁵/₈″ width; the trim allowance is included because the back will add about ¹/₈″.

My resonator is entirely faced with Brazilian rosewood veneer cut to a thickness of ¹/₄₀″. Both sides of the hoop, or wall, were faced in the initial lamination. The top edge was capped with an ebony and maple veneer sandwich in the same way as the rosewood tambourine. (See page 77.) The flat ebony face was inlaid with 4 mm green abalone dots spaced 1″ apart. Shallow holes were drilled just deep enough for the dots to protrude slightly. They were glued with epoxy and filed flush. The side face of the resonator was inlaid with pearl and abalone nested ³/₈″ squares spaced at 3¹/₂″ intervals. Inlay mortises were cut with a ¹/₄″ chisel. Epoxy was applied to the mortise and the nested edge of the pearl. A piece of plastic tape held the pieces in place while they dried.

The next day, a filler of powdered burnt umber mixed with epoxy was spread over crevices around all the inlay. Filling had to be done twice to fill all crevices, and when finally sanded smooth, looked like a flawlessly precise inlay job.

Using the same rosewood veneer, I made a four-ply back for the resonator. My rosewood was in four-inch strips and I first glued each strip to a cross-grain maple veneer backing with epoxy. All the strips were taped to prevent shifting and slip sheeted with freezer wrap before clamping overnight.

The strips were cleaned off and carefully trimmed with a sharp knife to book-match the veneers. They were taped together with one-inch plastic tape to hold the ensemble together. Both sides were prepared in this manner. Epoxy was applied to the strip joints by flexing the assembly, and a coat of epoxy was spread over one entire side. The two parts were placed together with the strips running at right angles to each other and then clamped between two discs (41).

39. Overall pattern of abalone dots lend sparkle to resonator back

40. Sawing ebony and maple veneer sandwich for resonator edging strips

Gluing the back to the resonator wall requires a special jig (44). Cut a 14″ disc of ³/₄″ pressed wood or plywood and draw on it a circle the exact inside diameter of your resonator wall. Glue eight small blocks against the inner edge of this circle so that when the resonator wall is dropped in place, it remains a true circle and stationary. Drill small lead holes around the disc edge at 1¹/₂″ intervals for roundhead 1¹/₂″ screws. Screw them in, leaving the unthreaded shank exposed. Purchase a box of four- or five-inch rubber bands.

The glued-up back was sanded smooth and a pattern of inlay dots laid out on the best face. These were drilled for 4 mm abalone dots. Because of the thinness of the rosewood veneer the final back thickness was ³/₃₂″. I used a ⁵/₃₂″ twist drill with the point filed to a shallow angle to drill the holes ³/₆₄″ deep. The dots were not set in place until after the back was glued to the resonator wall.

A block of wood with the top rounded off was set in the center of the resonator jig. This block was sized to produce a crown of about ¹/₄″ in the center. The gluing edge of the wall was filed to the appropriate angle and the back was glued in place with epoxy. If your back is very rigid, you can pre-dish it before gluing by inverting it on the resonator wall and placing a bag of sand or other weight in the center. Leave it for three or four days and then glue it in place.

With a purfling cutter a corner ledge was cut out for a binding strip of ebonized maple with a black-white strip on each side to go with the ebony and maple facing on the top edge. Black-white combination purfling strips are sold by guitar maker's supply houses. Bindings are also commonly made with plastic and ivoroid, an imitation of ivory. The completed binding was smoothed level with the resonator surface with a scraper blade and the corner was slightly rounded with fine sandpaper.

All the abalone dots were glued in place on the back, filled and carefully filed and sanded flush. A wash coat of white shellac (1 part shellac to 5 parts alcohol) was sprayed on the entire resonator with a mouth-blown atomizer, which consists of two thin tubes attached at right angles. To use the atomizer you blow through one tube with the other end in the liquid. This simple, cheap device is sold in art supply stores and was the traditional means of spraying charcoal drawings to keep them from smearing. I use it for wash coating and toning guitar tops with spirit varnish. On rosewood, spraying has the advantage of not causing bleeding onto lighter wood, which would happen if the shellac were applied by brush. Rosewood must always be

sealed or the varnish will not dry. And because it is an open-pored wood it must also be filled to provide a smooth surface for the final finish.

Filler is a mixture of ground quartz silex and pigment in a varnish-type vehicle, and comes in several colors. The color of the filler should be the same or slightly darker than the wood it will fill. Dig a lump of filler out of the can and thin it with benzene until it has the consistency of heavy cream. Brush it on parallel to the grain with a good bristle brush. Avoid getting it on the white purfling strips if you can. When the filler dries to a cloudy or fogged appearance—usually about twenty minutes—wipe off the excess filler with a coarse cotton cloth. Depending on how open the pores are, filling may have to be done twice to fill all the pores and provide a hard, smooth base for finishing. The final finish can be no better than the surface underneath.

Before any finish is applied to the resonator, the filler must be absolutely dry. Laying a finish on a partly dry filler is a common finishing hazard. The finish will not dry—necessitating removal of all fin-

42. *Filing off epoxy filler on side inlay*

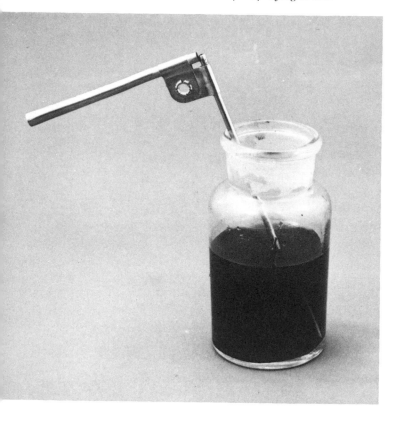

43. Mouth blow-tube makes simple spraying device

ishing materials down to the wood and starting all over again. Allow a day, preferably two, for drying filler.

Lightly sand the dried surface until smooth and spray or brush on another wash coat of shellac. If the white purfling strips have gotten muddied by filler, lightly scrape them clean with a single-edge razor. Apply six coats of polyurethane varnish, scuff sanding between coats, and with one day's drying time between coats. Four or five days after the last coat, the surface can be smoothed with #400 wet-or-dry sandpaper and water. Dip a folded piece of the paper into water and carefully smooth away all lumps and unevenness. After initial smoothing has been accomplished, change to #600 paper. Use enough water to lubricate and float off the pulverized finish while polishing in a small circular motion. Clean off the surface with a dry cloth and inspect frequently as polishing proceeds. Be extra careful when sanding corner edges, the easiest place to go through the finish. A final high finish is achieved by rubbing with Duco #7 Auto Polishing liquid and a felt pad.

The inside of the resonator need not receive more than two coats of varnish and does not have to be polished.

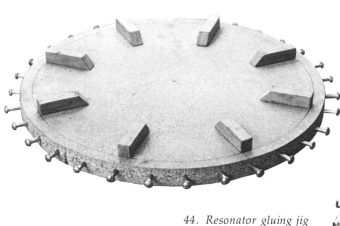

44. Resonator gluing jig with back under pressure

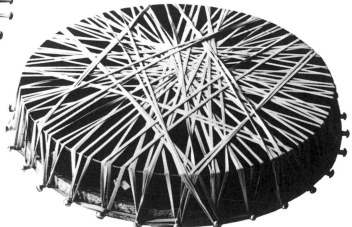

45. *Nickel-silver flange sections resting on sawing support*

Flange

Banjos having resonators use an openwork metal flange as a decorative fascia to conceal the trough between shell and resonator and to secure the resonator to the shell. Sound waves reflected from the arched resonator back exit through the pierced openings in the flange. Manufactured flanges are normally castings or stampings which are then plated.

Nickel silver is the best choice for making your own flange. It is not much more expensive than brass, looks like silver, and has high tarnish resistance. If you later decide to have it chromed or gold plated, nickel silver is easily plated. Sheet brass can also be used for cutting a flange but unless it is coated with a clear lacquer or plated, it will tarnish. Most banjo parts come nickel or chrome plated to prevent tarnishing.

A piece of 8" x 10" fourteen-gauge sheet brass or nickel silver will suffice for cutting a four-piece flange. Start by drawing an accurate half-section plan of your shell and resonator. Use the full width of the trough between shell and resonator for the flange. By the time you saw out the sections and file the rough edges smooth, your flange will probably drop in place with some slight clearance. In any case you can always file it down to fit.

If you are using a notched tension hoop, spot the holes for the hooks in your flange drawing. These holes must be accurately placed to ensure that all the hooks rise perpendicularly to properly engage their notch. If you are using a V-groove tension hoop with flat hooks, there is no problem with vertical rise.

Openwork designs that make strategic use of drilled holes are the easiest to make. Fig. 49 shows some patterns that can be made with simple saw

46. *Full-size plan for banjo flange*

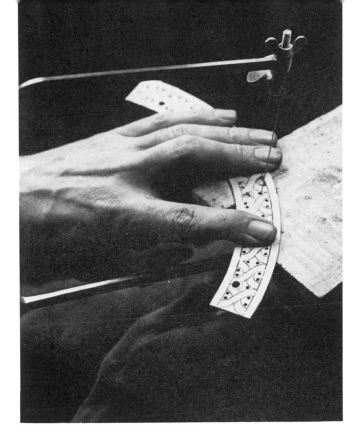

cuts linking drill holes. Flanges can be made with just a pattern of drill holes but tend to look mechanical and uninteresting. A flange, after all, is the most striking element on a resonator banjo and merits artistic consideration. A hand-cut flange of some attractive intricacy is what most immediately distinguishes a custom banjo from the ordinary commercial banjo.

The interwoven motif I used on my flange is all cut out with a jeweler's saw. I began by coating a sheet of fourteen-gauge nickel silver with a light spray coat of matte white paint (aerosol). One half of the flange was drawn on tracing paper and then transferred to the sprayed surface using nonsmudge carbon paper and a 4H pencil. The tracing was then reversed and the other half traced down. I sprayed the tracing lightly with clear acrylic spray (Krylon) to prevent smudging. The tracing can also be darkened with waterproof India ink to preserve legibility during handling. Note that the top quarter sections have an area left clear to allow for the heel cutout.

Small holes were drilled in each segment to be cut out so that the saw blade could be inserted. Additional small holes were drilled to facilitate the cutting of corners and general maneuvering of the saw. Because of the length of the quarter sections, a jeweler's saw with a six-inch depth was used to permit free rotation of the sections even when working in the middle. The saw blade used was a Herkules 2/0, which is strong enough to support the weight of a section when the upper end of the blade is secured. Saw teeth rake downward, and the frame must be squeezed together before securing the blade to ensure enough tension to keep the blade rigid while sawing.

Sawing action is almost vertical, using a steady, rhythmic motion, bearing in mind that the saw cuts only on the downstroke. Corners are negotiated by sawing in one place while the work is slowly turned until forward sawing motion can be resumed. Blades are fragile and any sudden twist will snap them. Jewelers use a cake of beeswax to lubricate the saw blade for easier cutting. The cake is nailed to the workbench and the saw blade run through it

48. Resting flange section near handle while securing saw blade

43

occasionally while sawing.

After sawing is completed, all rough edges are filed smooth. Polish the top surface with crocus cloth. Pressing the crocus cloth into the pierced openings while polishing will round off the edges slightly, increasing the play of light over the surface. A finer degree of polish can be imparted with a felt disc charged with tripoli or green rouge. For a high mirror finish after all surface scratches have been polished out, use a muslin buffing wheel charged with rouge. Apply polishing compound sparingly to avoid buildup. After polishing, clean up all greasy residue by scrubbing the sections in hot water and detergent with a small amount of ammonia added. A discarded toothbrush will help to

get out the polishing compound lodged in narrow crevices.

Flanges can be engraved with an electric vibrating tool that will sort of jiggle an image into the metal. This is a shortcut method of engraving and bears only a faint resemblance to the engraving done on silverware with a burin or graver. Engraved designs break up the surface with an attractive play of light and introduce a note of antique elegance.

On my flange I wanted to accentuate the interwoven character of the design and used two methods to accomplish this: a spot-plating technique using a stop-off lacquer combined with a pattern of closely spaced engraved lines oriented to catch the light from different directions.

First, I painted on a stop-off lacquer, coating everything but one half of the interwoven motif. Stop-off lacquers are formulated to resist the heat of the plating process and keep coated areas free of plating. The lacquer (obtained from the electroplater) was applied with a small artist's brush. Thin areas were coated twice and the four flange sections were then gold plated.

The lacquer was peeled off easily and gold that managed to bleed onto unwanted areas was polished out. A pattern of cross-hatched lines was then engraved on the other half of the interwoven motif. The lines were scratched in with a tungsten-carbide-tipped scribing pencil using a small, transparent plastic triangle as a guide. Precision in ruling the lines is unimportant. The orientation of the lines working around a circle means that some portions of the flange will always be reflecting light and the unreflecting engraved portions will appear matte.

The total visual effect of the interwoven design was greatly improved by the difference between the gold and the textured quality of the engraved surface. Even without gold plating, the contrast would be striking. Polishing of the gold was done by burnishing with an agate burnisher, a process that removes no gold. Before the flange sections were installed, they were washed with hot water, detergent, and some ammonia, and polished dry with a clean flannel cloth.

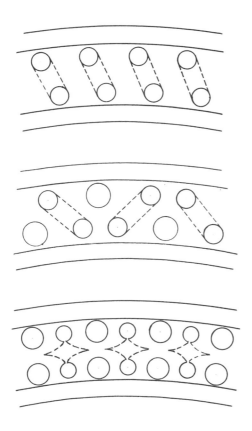

49. Simple flange designs using drill holes

50. *Testing fit of flange to make sure it does not bind on resonator wall*

Fitting Resonator to Banjo

The banjo must be completely assembled with flange in place to mount the resonator. Situate the neck heel where you want it on the resonator and cut out a portion of the resonator wall to match the shape of the heel. Cut it close fitting and gradually file it to a looser fit to accommodate a strip of felt as a cushion. When the heel is seated, the flange should be about 1/8" below the rim of the resonator. Glue in the felt strip and seat the banjo in place with a prop under the shell to level the flange where

it should be. Mark off on the resonator rim the exact position of the thumbscrew holes in the flange. Drill the four shallow holes that receive the wall lugs 3/8" below the top edge of the rim. I used a small hand drill to drill these holes, the kind that stores drills in the handle. By removing the screw cap of the handle, I just managed to get it into the resonator horizontally. I also cut off 1/16" of the wall lug screw because my wall thickness was a bit under 3/8", 11/32" to be exact. I was afraid that a deeper hole coincident with an inlay portion might split the wood. Screw in the wall lugs, position the banjo and flange in the resonator, and put in the thumbscrews.

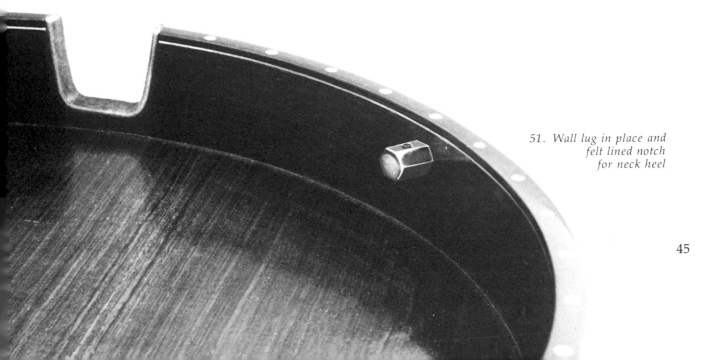

51. *Wall lug in place and felt lined notch for neck heel*

45

52. Ebony faced head with pearl,
abalone, and brass inlay

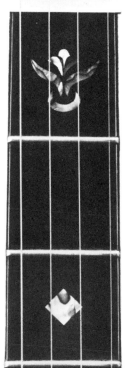

Inlay

Traditionally, banjos have been adorned with mother-of-pearl and abalone inlay. A variety of pre-cut pearl designs is available in various shapes and sizes but these are expensive. For the craftsman with an artistic bent and a penchant for small-scale, patient endeavor, cutting pearl inlay will present no problem, Learning to use the jeweler's saw is the key.

Pearl and abalone are sold in rectangular blanks ranging up to about 1" x 2" and about $1/16$" thick. Pearl almost always is a pearlescent white but abalone comes in a basically green or red coloration with vivid contrasts in pattern and color. Colors range over the entire spectrum with gemlike iridescence. Refraction is high but directional; rotating a piece will obscure its brilliance and abalone should be positioned with this in mind. Its layered structure also means that sanding may change that brilliant chartreuse you admired to a pale watery green.

Begin by preparing a pencil sketch of your design on tracing paper. Sand the pearl smooth with fine garnet paper or #400 wet-or-dry paper. Trace

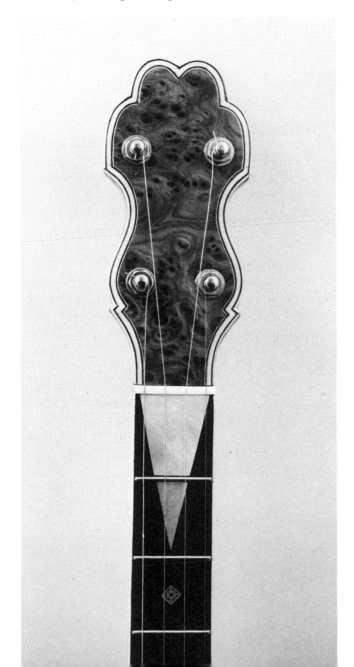

53. Burl faced head with ivoroid and black plastic edge binding

down the design using nonsmudge carbon paper and a 4H pencil. If you are tracing onto a vividly colored piece of abalone, first spray the surface with a light coat of matte white (aerosol). If you tend to smudge the tracing while sawing, it can be fixed with a spray coat of clear Krylon.

Position all intricate pieces with their most delicate portions along the edge of the pearl blank. Use a 2/0 or finer blade and saw out these delicate parts first. This will enable you to safely file fragile appendages while still attached to the pearl blank.

All sawing is done over a keyhole sawing platform (45) so that pieces are adequately supported while being sawed. Saw slowly, rhythmically without any abrupt turns or twists. If the saw jams, release the top end of the blade and pull it down and out of the saw kerf, a better solution than breaking the piece or the blade by forcing. Breaking blades is a common hazard for beginner and expert alike, which is why jewelers buy blades by the gross.

A clean break in a piece of inlay can be glued together with epoxy or Duco cement. Position the glued pieces on a piece of Scotch tape to hold them together while gluing. Six-inch half-round and round files are the ones I use most for smoothing rough edges. Pearl inlay looks best when all contours are smooth and sharp.

Glue the cutout piece of inlay in position on the surface where it will be inlaid. Use only a tiny dab of white glue to immobilize the piece while being traced. A piece with a simple shape can be held in place with the eraser end of a pencil while being traced. On elaborate designs such as the Sho-boat banjo head, all the pieces were glued in placed before being traced. This permits final adjustments in the positioning of pieces to gain the best overall effect. Tracing is done with a sharp-pointed 6H pencil, working right up against the pearl contour. Tape some strips of masking tape to a board with enough adhesive surface exposed to hold all the inlay pieces. Gently sever the glue joint under each piece with a single-edge razor blade, and transfer each piece to the masking tape with a tweezer.

I use a Dremel Moto-Tool with a shaper base to cut the inlay mortise. For fine work I use the #111

47

54. *Head facing veneer sandwich with all inlay lightly glued in place on surface*

55. *Dremel Moto-Tool with shaper base*

router bit sold as a Dremel accessory. Sample cuts are tried on a scrap piece of wood until the cutter depth leaves the pearl a hair above the surrounding surface. If you are mixing pearl and abalone, the cutter will have to be set to the depth of the thinnest material; abalone is often cut thinner than pearl.

I skim the cutter just under the surface of the wood to fix the contour. Gently continuing with this skimming technique, I gradually work the cutter deeper and deeper until the shaper base is resting flat and the full depth has been cut. If you try to cut to full depth at once, the small cutter will overheat and quickly dull. Another way to rout the mortise would be to set the cutter at half the depth and lower the cutter for the final cut.

Try the inlay for fit in the routed mortise. Use fine-pointed tweezers to handle the pieces, exercising care in lifting them in and out of the mortise. If you tilt a piece while lifting it out, it may jam and break.

After all the pieces are fitted, daub some clear epoxy into the bottom of each mortise. Press the inlay pieces into place and jog them into proper alignment. Leave overnight to dry.

For inlay on ebony, fill all crevices with epoxy colored with powdered lampblack. Press it in with a small spatula or knife and leave overnight. Sand the inlay areas smooth with #100 garnet paper wrapped around a wooden block to minimize the tendency of the softer wood to wear away faster than the pearl. If there are any holes in the filled areas, repeat the filler step again. Final smoothing of inlaid areas can be done with a single-edge razor blade used as a scraper and a final going-over with fine garnet paper. For maximum brilliance, pearl should be free of all scratches.

Epoxy filler can be blended with powdered pigments to match any wood shade. Earth colors—raw and burnt umbers and siennas—plus Van Dyke brown are excellent for mixing almost any shade of wood. These powdered pigments and lampblack are sold in any good art supply store. All can be mixed with clear epoxy to make an invisible join between inlay and surrounding surface.

For inlay patterns that cross fret slots, the pearl

cannot be cut right up to the slot. If a 1/32" buffer strip of wood is not left between the slot and the pearl, the fret wire's studded tang will chip and fracture the pearl. The buffer stip will anchor the fret wire and protect the brittle pearl. The visual effect of the pearl design crossing the frets will not be spoiled. On old banjos this was not a problem because until the early 1930's, fret wire was an unstudded metal strip of uniform thickness.

On the Sho-boat banjo head I also make use of brass inlay. I used twenty-six gauge sheet traced and cut out in the same way as the pearl inlay. Brass, nickel silver, and copper can be inlaid in any area that will be varnished.

56. *After all inlay was completed, the contour was sawed out in one precise, continuous line with a jeweler's saw. The exterior cutoff section was set aside and the sawed contour lightly smoothed. Thin strips of 26 gauge brass were bent to exact shape using parallel and needle nose pliers. When the entire contour was fitted with brass strips, the exterior section was dropped over the whole to check fit. When a good fit was achieved, the brass strips were simultaneously glued in place with the exterior section. Epoxy mixed with lampblack was used to glue and the outer section was pressed firmly against the brass lined contour with push pins pressed into a backing board alongside the exterior section. When dry, an outline parallel to the brass contour was drawn in and sawed out to get the finished shape of the head.*

49

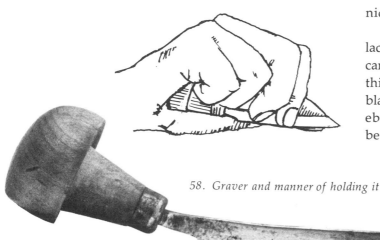

57. Engraved pearl inlay is an old banjo tradition

Engraving

Pearl can be engraved with incised lines that can be filled with blacking to add design and textural interest to pearl inlay. Engraving is done with a graver, or burin, and practice is necessary to gain control. Pearl is brittle and grainy because of its layered structure, and making straight or curved lines on its surface is not an easy matter.

Hold the graver—lozenge or half-point cutter is best for pearl—with the handle in the hollow of the palm, the bent fingers on the front edge of the blade, the extended thumb on the other side, and the little finger fitted into the hollow of the handle. This is the traditional technique for wood engraving and also works for pearl although more pressure is required. The main virtue of this method of holding and guiding the graver is that it gives great control because the thumb is always in contact with the surface being engraved. Curved lines are engraved by mounting the inlay on a block of wood and turning the block as the graver cuts.

Holding the graver like a chisel and pushing it away from you leaves you without the control necessary to make designs of any intricacy and also presents the danger of slipping. A study of old banjo pearl engraving reveals that the men who did this work were well versed in the traditional techniques of the wood engraver.

Incised lines can be blacked by wiping on black lacquer. When the lacquer dries, the top surfaces can be cleaned with a cloth moistened in lacquer thinner. Blacking can also be done with the lampblack and epoxy filler mixture used to fill crevices in ebony. When it dries in the lines, the surfaces can be cleaned with fine sandpaper.

58. Graver and manner of holding it

Tailpiece and Arm Rest

It is not practical to make an adjustable tailpiece since they are available cheaply, and the same holds true for arm rests. It is possible, however, to transform these accessories into something more distinctive through the application of attractive metal overlays incorporating pearl or abalone inlay.

On the Sho-boat tailpiece, a standard adjustable model, I first cut a small square of fourteen-gauge nickel silver into a pierced design. Pearl was fitted to the corner cutouts and a piece of abalone fitted to the center cutout. When all the inlay pieces were precisely fitted, the pierced metal appliqué was soft-soldered to the tailpiece cover. The heat generated in soft-soldering will not damage the tailpiece. The cooled piece was scrubbed with hot water to clean off dried flux, and the inlay pieces were glued in place with epoxy. The nickel silver appliqué was filed down flush with the inlay and the entire cover buffed with a felt wheel charged with tripoli. Filing and polishing must be done carefully to avoid removing the plating, which would mean replating. Nickel and chrome plating are surprisingly durable and it takes a fair amount of polishing to go through the plating.

The arm rest I used is a Stewart-MacDonald Company catalog item. A long section was cut out of the top face, leaving a 3/16″ margin of metal all around. This curved opening was filed smooth and traced onto 1/8″ maple plywood. Four oversize strips of pearl were fitted over this tracing and glued in place with white glue. In this case the metal was thinner than the pearl and the pearl was filed and sanded to the exact thickness of the metal border. Filing is not possible after the inlay is glued in place without removing the plating. The cutout portion was traced down on the pearl assembly and the shape cut out with a jeweler's saw.

A piece of fourteen-gauge nickel silver was cut out to the shape of the top face of the arm rest. After making sure the edge contour matched the arm rest, the piece was soft-soldered to the underside of the top face. The pearl was soaked off the plywood with hot water and reassembled in the cavity. When the pieces were exactly fitted to the cavity, they were glued in place with epoxy.

In this form of appliqué decoration, the inlay must be a tight fit because there is no attractive way of filling a gap between pearl and metal. Interesting variations are possible using ebony or ivory inlay. Brass can also be used for inlaying on nickel silver.

51

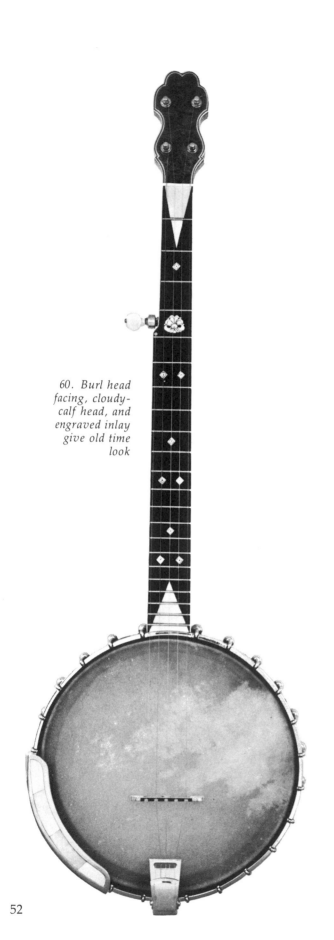

60. Burl head facing, cloudy-calf head, and engraved inlay give old time look

61. Neck lag bolts secure neck to shell

Assembly and Tuning Pegs

Put together the complete body assembly (minus flange, resonator, tailpiece, or arm rest) and screw the head down to playing tension. Make sure the tension hoop is level all around the rim. Position the neck against the back of the shell so that the fretboard face is level with the bottom of the string clearance cutout in the tension hoop. Mark where the bottom of the flesh hoop falls, on the side of the neck. Mark a horizontal line across the front end of the neck 1/8" below the flesh hoop mark. Chisel out and smooth the large recess above the line that provides clearance for the flesh hoop and tension hoop. Curve this recess to conform to the curve of the tension hoop and hollow out the end face of the neck to conform to the curve of the shell. Use files, round scraper blade, and sandpaper to get this curve right. When it sets flush against the shell without rocking and with adequate clearance for hoop movement, it is ready for joining to the shell.

Stand the body on edge with the bottom portion of the shell resting on the workbench. Stand the neck upright in position on the shell exactly centered on the string clearance cutout. Reach a long-pointed pencil through the neck bolt holes and mark

62. *Inlaid arm rest and tailpiece accentuate custom appearance*

the hole positions on the end face of the neck.

I use standard banjo neck bolts with lag bolt thread on one end, 10/24 machine thread on the other end and hex nut. Drill the holes in the neck a size smaller than the lag bolt thread so that it will screw in. Screwing in the bolt can be made easier by threading on a hex nut and then threading on another so that it jams against the first nut. The bolt can then be screwed in with a $^5/_{16}''$ bracket wrench on the top nut. If you are screwing into the center joint of a glued-up neck, apply a clamp to the sides of the neck where you are screwing.

With both bolts in place, fasten the neck to the shell. Check the neck for alignment with a long straightedge. If it is off, a compensatory amount of wood must be removed from one side of the front end.

Remove the neck and drill the four $^3/_8''$ holes for the tuning pegs. I use Five Star Planet tuning pegs and companion fifth peg. These have a 4:1 gear ratio and adjustable spring tension. For the fifth peg, which has a tapered end housing, I drilled a $^1/_4''$ hole and reamed it with a cut-down #2 Morse taper pin reamer. When the tapered housing could go in al-

most all the way to the stop, I smeared a mixture of fine sawdust and Titebond in the hole and pressed home the peg. Drill a small lead hole above the fifth fret for the small roundhead screw that acts as a nut for the fifth string. Use a nonferrous screw.

Attach the tailpiece and string up the banjo. Strike the harmonic at the twelfth fret to find the position of the bridge. When the pitch of the fingered note at the twelfth fret coincides with the harmonic, make a small pencil mark on the head just in front of each foot. Adjust the string height, if necessary, by switching to a lower or higher bridge or by changing the angle slightly on the end face of the neck.

On the Sho-boat banjo I use a bridge made of ivory. Ivory is rigid enough to dispense with a center foot in the bridge, a feature I dislike, and I also wanted a longer bridge. From an acoustic standpoint, I feel most banjo bridges are too short.

63. Henry Potter & Co., London 1885 (Belgian Royal Army Museum)

Regimental Snare Drum

During Britain's golden age of empire, her soldiers marched across distant battlefields to the percussive rattle of a snare drum. Regimental drummers carried drums bearing the royal crest and battle honors into the Crimea, Burma, India, South Africa, and the Sudan. Besides being a colorful symbol of empire, regimental drums offer a terse chronology of nineteenth-century British military history in the campaign listings on their sides.

Drummers were young men trained to beat a brisk march tempo and double on bugle when necessary. They were esteemed for their mastery of the drum roll, a sustained percussive effect whose quality of awesome foreboding is powerfully evoked in Oscar Wilde's poem "The Ballad of Reading Gaol." The drums themselves were important sentimental possessions of the regiment and their loss by enemy capture was counted a grave misfortune. Leather braces, drum slings, and, occasionally, ropes were kept white with a tin of Blanco, a pipe clay and chalk compound. In off-hours, a drum served as a convenient card table or desk for letter writing.

Snare drums developed from the medieval tabor, a double-headed, rope-tensioned drum of varying size with a single snare on the batter head. Tabors were often played in combination with pipes, the tabor slung at the waist and struck with a stick held in the right hand while the pipe was fingered with the left hand. The early existence of this pairing of drum with fife is recorded in the *Chronicles of the City of Basle* for 1322. By the sixteenth century, the snare drum had emerged as a military instrument associated with the infantry and the fife.

Early drum shells were made of oak, beech, or ash, but by the mid-nineteenth century military snare drums were being made of brass. An historically important manufacturer and supplier of drums to the British army has been Henry Potter & Company in Aldershot, a major center of army activity in England. Potter's has been in existence since 1742 and is still making drums. My own researches into the snare drum have focused mainly on a large collection of nineteenth-century Potter drums at the Belgian Royal Army Museum in Brussels and a number of earlier drums at the National Army Museum in London.

64. Foot guard regiment side drum, no snare, wooden shell with tacked pattern, c. 1815 (National Army Museum, London)

65. H. Potter & Co., c. 1910. Tab braces reversed, normally face left. (Belgian Royal Army Museum)

Regulation guard pattern drum:

Brass shell: 13 3/4" x 11 1/2"
Hoops: 14 5/8" x 1 5/8" x 3/8", ten holes
Snare: Six strand gut

Note: A set of counter and flesh hoops for this drum uses about 22 sq. ft. of veneer for lamination.

Metal Shell Construction

Sheet brass is the best choice for snare drum construction because it is easily soldered and painted and will make an attractive drum without any surface decoration. Copper is too soft, and aluminum is difficult to solder or braze and will not make as good a drum.

Half-hard twenty-one gauge (.029″) brass is a good thickness to work with and can be purchased from a 10″ roll. Half-hard twenty-gauge (.032″) is heavier but is available from 6″, 8″, 10″, or 12″ rolls. These widths are also available in sheet with a minimum length of 8′. If you order by mail there is a good chance the brass will arrive in a roll.

A $^1/_{16}$″ space must be left between hoop and shell to allow for the skin thickness, which means that the outside diameter of the shell will be $^1/_8$″

66. Jig for soft soldering inside seam strip, clamping board faced with asbestos.

smaller than the inside diameter of the hoops. Multiply the shell diameter by 3.141 (π) to find the length of flat sheet required. Add one inch to this length for a seam strip, which will be cut off. A $13^3/_4$″ diameter shell requires a flat sheet $43^3/_{16}$″ long plus one inch for the seam strip, making a total of $44^3/_{16}$″. Double-check this size by cutting a $43^3/_{16}$″ strip of veneer. Bend it into a butted circle and glue a shorter strip behind the joint to hold it together. Drop this circle inside the counter hoop to make sure that you have at least $^1/_{16}$″ clearance. Too little clearance will constrict the free movement of the skins over the shell rim; too much clearance makes a sloppy drum with a tendency for the hoops to get tilted out of alignment.

Cut off the one-inch seam strip from your sheet of brass with a saw or shears. If you can get your supplier to chop off the seam strip, so much the better. If you must saw or shear the metal, try to avoid the kind of deformation that will require hammering to straighten. Some waviness is unavoidable but can usually be straightened by simple hand pressure. Hammering, unless you are expert, will leave dents.

Roll the brass sheet into as tight a cylinder as you can without making any sudden or sharp bends, so that it will unroll to roughly the cylindrical shape it will assume. This will permit checking the butt joint of the ends without fighting the tension of the metal. File the two edges so that they butt neatly together.

Cut off a $^3/_8$″ strip from one end of the seam strip to allow for the reinforcing rings that will solder to the rims of the shell. With emery cloth (medium grit) sand the back of the butted joint and one side of the seam strip. Sand these soldering areas shiny bright and avoid fingering them.

Face a $^3/_4$″ x 6″ x 13″ piece of plywood with a sheet of $^1/_8$″ asbestos. Roll the shell into a butted cylinder and position it on the asbestos with the butted joint centered on the board. Put a few drops of flux on the back of the seam strip and position it over the butted shell joint. Clamp it in place with an aluminum bar and two clamps (66).

Use a medium burner tip on your propane

67. *Completed shell with painting begun around letters*

68. Author's copy of Belgian army snare drum, c. 1890:

Brass shell: 12¹³/₁₆″ x 6³/₈″
Hoops: 13½″ x 1½″ x ¹¹/₃₂″, fifteen holes
Snare: Double strand gut

torch and heat the seam strip to soldering temperature with a brisk flame. Concentrate the flame over a four- or five-inch section of the seam joint. When the solder begins to melt, draw it along the joint until it is sealed. The heated seam strip and capillary action will draw the melted solder into the joint and throughout the seam strip area. Soldering will go smoothly if all surfaces are absolutely clean and held in close contact by clamps. Heat the area to be soldered—not the solder—and remember that solder cannot flow into a joint that has not been adequately coated with flux. After the joint cools, remove the clamps and check the joint on both sides of the shell. Wash off dried flux with a brush and hot water.

Bend a ¼″ x 48″ brass rod into a circle the size of the shell. When the rod conforms to the circle of the shell, clamp it to the inside of the shell just under the rim. Use two more clamps to hold the ring in place while you mark the cutoff spot. Do this with great care to ensure that the ring, after it is brazed together, will just fit the rim with gentle forcing.

Remove the ring and saw through your mark. Save the cutoff piece. If you started with two brass rods exactly 48″ in length, you can simply cut an identically sized piece off the second rod after you have bent it into a circle. Bend the ends of your cutoff rod past each other so that they can be sprung into a butt joint. Before applying flux be sure that both ends are in tight contact over their entire surface. If you prop the ring on some charcoal blocks (jeweler's item), you can use small tacks or nails to hold the joint together (26). Braze with a brass composition rod, the appropriate flux, and a large burner tip. Hard silver solder can also be used. A large, brisk flame is necessary to bring the brass up to the high temperature necessary for brazing or hard-soldering. The joint must be closed with a high-temperature weld so that it will not spring open when the ring is soldered into the shell.

File the finished joint into a smooth continuity with the rest of the ring. With emery cloth polish smooth the outer edge of the ring and the inner edge of the shell rim where the ring will join. Press the ring into place with its top half protruding above the shell rim, and use four or five small clamps to hold it in place. This rounded edge is important as a support for the skin head, which is constantly moving under hoop pressure each time the ropes are tensioned. Apply flux to a six-inch section and soft-solder the ring to the rim with a fine

58

burner tip. Work your way around the rim, skipping the clamps, and being careful to maintain the same amount of ring protruding above the rim. Finally, remove the clamps and solder those missing spots. Solder in the other ring in the same manner. Wash off dried flux with a brush and hot water.

The key to success in soldering the rings is a press fit. If a ring is loose enough to fall to the bottom of the shell, it must be cut open and a small piece of rod brazed in place to give the needed fit. Solder will not fill the gaps in a loose fit. If the poor fit is a result of the ring not being round enough, stand the ring up on a hard surface and hammer the inside of the ring with a domed face hammer. Keep turning the ring and hammering until it is round.

After both rings are in, file and sand with fine emery paper all edges around the shell rim that might snag or abrade the skins. Drill a $3/8''$ air hole in the center of the shell right through the butted joint. Air holes prevent acoustic "loading" of a drum that would interfere with the proper vibration of the heads. Holes vary in size from about $3/8''$ for a snare drum to $5/8''$ or more for a bass drum. The hole can be anywhere on the shell but is usually placed behind or above the snare jack housing. Do not put the hole where it is apt to be covered by the drummer's body.

The snare jack mechanism (also called snare strainer) controls the tension of the snares against the snare head, and its location on the shell is influenced by the character of the roping and the depth of the shell. If the shell is 10" or 12" deep (about the limit for a snare drum) the jack is normally located in the lower half of the shell close to the snare bed. On shallow snare drums the jack is centered on the shell. The snare stud is fastened in the same location on the opposite side of the shell. The jack itself must be scaled to a size that will not bring it into awkward proximity with the ropes; it must be clear of the braces when they are at playing tension halfway down the side. Tenor drums have no snare and the deeper a drum is, the farther down on the ropes will be the position of playing tension for the braces.

Modern snare drums employ a quick-action snare-adjusting device but older drums used some form of screw tensioning that required fresh adjustment each time the snare was used. Nineteenth-century Belgian and Dutch drums often used a decoratively contoured housing (73). Tightening a wing nut raises the screw to which the gut snares are attached. The screw itself cannot turn because its bottom end is square and let into a square cutout.

The jack on both the Belgian drum and the Fife drum was made of sheet brass and $1/4''$ threaded brass rod. It was assembled with hard solder and soft-soldered in position on the shell. The snare studs were cut from sheet brass and rod, hard-soldered together, and then filed to shape. A better way to make a stud is to turn it on a lathe. Before soft-soldering the jack or stud to the shell, its back must be filed slightly concave to match the curve of the shell.

69. Two styles of Potter snare jacks

59

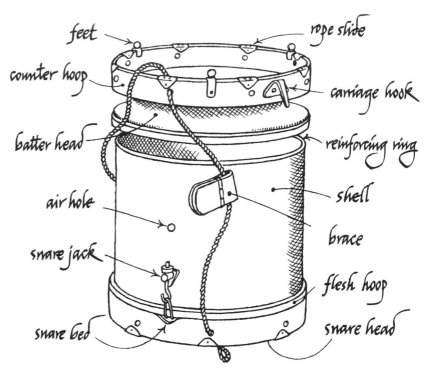

feet · rope slide · counter hoop · carriage hook · batter head · reinforcing ring · air hole · shell · snare jack · brace · flesh hoop · snare bed · snare head

Hoops and Snares

70. Drum parts

Counter hoops ride on the skin-wrapped flesh hoops and are held firmly in place by the shell and the roping through the hoops. When rope tension is increased by pushing down the leather braces, the counter hoops press down the flesh hoops, thus stretching taut the skins.

Counter and flesh hoops are laminations of eleven strips of maple veneer of standard thickness ($1/28''$). Ten strips glued into five cross-banded double strips plus one long-grain inner facing strip comprise the lamination of a hoop. (See Lamination Procedure, page 17.) Final hoop thickness will be about $3/8''$. The two flesh hoops are cut from a counter hoop, which means three counter hoops must be made for a drum. Three flesh hoops can actually be cut from a counter hoop because they are $7/16''$ in height. If you make two drums you will only have to make two hoops for a third drum because you will have accumulated two flesh hoops. Cut laminating strips at least $1/16''$ oversize to allow for final trimming.

Rope holes are spaced equidistantly in the rope hoops, drilled with a $9/32''$ drill for a 6 mm (approxi-

mately $15/64''$) rope. Drill holes are canted to follow the lie of the rope. Because of this angle, the drill holes are started slightly below the center of the hoop. Holes are drilled at a vertical angle of 45 degrees and canting them sideways is unnecessary. Use a caul to protect against fracturing the inner face veneer when the drill exits. Twist a piece of #100 garnet paper into a small pointed shape and use it in the manner of a countersink to round smooth the entrance and exit of each hole.

The snare bed is cut out on opposite sides of the snare hoop to permit running the snares across the snare head. On the Belgian drum (68) the snare bed is actually a half-moon-shaped hole cut into the hoop. This design requires a deep collar on the snare head so that the snare action is not obstructed. This drum also has an odd number of rope holes (fifteen), which means one of the snare bed cutouts falls where a hole should be. This problem was handled by the use of a hook-end bracket as a substitute for a hole.

Snares were traditionally gut and ranged in number from two to eight strands, made by dou-

71. *Drum hoop release form uses two pegs along each quadrant*

72. *Gut snares on Potter drum*

bling a single strand back and forth. Gut is getting scarce but is still used for stringing tennis rackets, harps, 'cellos, and bass viols. A diameter of $^5/_{64}''$ appears to have been the standard. Modern snare drums use snares made of nylon, wire, or wire-covered silk. James Blades, the renowned English percussionist, states in his fine book (*Percussion Instruments and Their History*) that "gut snares impart a true military sound."

Warming gut in the sun or on a warm radiator will soften it to a more workable pliancy. Make a small loop in one end by whipping with thread or fine wire to avoid a knot. Slip this loop over the snare stud, pass the rest through the snare bed, across the snare head, through the opposite snare bed, loop over the snare jack hook, and back to the snare stud via the same route. Wet the end of the gut strand to soften it so that it can easily be knotted to tie off the gut at the snare stud. At this point, the snares should lie close enough to the snare head so that a few turns on the jack screw will bring them up to playing tension. Attaching the snares is the last thing done after assembling the drum.

73. *Snare jack housing and outrigger hook on Belgian drum*

61

Drum Heads and Lapping

74. *Worker cutting calf drum head in skin loft at H. Band & Co., Ltd.*

Calfskin heads are sold in two basic grades of roughly three weights—light, medium, and heavy. The best grades of calf heads are firm in texture, of uniform thickness, free of blemishes, and almost white. Heads are also available in a less expensive cloudy-calf grade processed with less finish and closer to a natural rawhide condition. They bear pigmented areas showing vaguely the animal color markings and traces of hair occasionally remain. I use these skins because they are cheaper although they sometimes pose more difficulty in mounting. Skins are a major cost item in drum building.

A medium-weight skin is best for a snare drum batter head that will see parade service. Snare heads should be thinner than the batter head to give a crisper, brighter sound.

Lapping—tucking the skins around the flesh hoop—is one of those jobs where descriptive words fall emphatically short of experience. Skins vary so in their physical characteristics, depending on the age of the animal, from what portion of the hide the skin is cut, and how long the skin has been stored, that a description can at best only serve as a general guide.

A fourteen- or fifteen-inch overall diameter flesh hoop of $3/8''$ width x $7/16''$ height requires a $2^1/2''$ margin all around, that is, a fourteen-inch flesh hoop needs a nineteen-inch skin. This margin must cover the wrapping of the flesh hoop, the collar, and some shrinkage. Begin by cutting a cardboard circle to whatever size your flesh hoop requires. Place this pattern in the center of your skin and trace the contour with a soft pencil. Cut the skin head out with sharp scissors or a single-edge razor blade. Soak the head in a bathtub filled with enough cold water to submerge the skin. Under no circumstance should hot water be used because it will shrivel and distort the skin beyond redemption. Soak the skin for twelve to fifteen minutes.

A clean, nonabsorbent surface such as glass, marble, Formica, or the like will make a good working surface for lapping. Have handy two dozen spring clothespins and a lapping tool which is nothing more than a metal strip with the end bent over.

75. *Inverted saucer under center of skin helps control slack during lapping*

A smooth round tablespoon handle will also do the job.

Remove the skin from the bath. If it does not feel pliable enough to work with, soak for a few more minutes. When ready, remove the skin and towel off the excess moisture. Lay it smooth side down on the work surface and let it dry for ten minutes. If you have soaked the skin for too long you may have to wait a half hour. Before tucking the skin, it must reach that optimal state of suppleness which will permit tucking without fighting the stiffness of the skin but must not be so supple that the skin becomes doughy. When the skin becomes doughy, it is more liable to tear and stretch, and less likely to result in a neat lapping.

Center the flesh hoop on the skin and tuck a two-inch section. Get the lap right up to the inner edge and snug against the flesh hoop. Apply a clothespin to hold the tuck in place. Do the same thing diametrically opposite this tuck. Continue tucking in this manner until all the edge is tucked. Avoid any stretching that might pull the hoop out of shape. Some professionals use a slat cut to the out-side diameter of the hoop to check periodically that the flesh hoop remains a true circle.

When the edge is lapped, check to make sure that all is snugly in place. A bit of judicious chivying and coaxing should smooth away wrinkles, especially on the outer face of the flesh hoop, the part that is mainly visible on the assembled drum. Leave the clothespins on until the skin is sufficiently set to remove them safely, normally about a half hour. If the clothespins press too tightly or are left on too long, they will glue the skin to the flesh hoop at their point of contact, leaving a series of slightly darker spots. If this bothers you, you can avoid the problem by using larger metal spring clamps that can be clamped to the top and bottom surfaces of the flesh hoops where the spots are not noticeable. Skins contain glue and this helps secure the skin to the wood flesh hoop.

Fill a small flannel square with powdered chalk or talc, draw the edges of the square together, and secure tightly with a rubber band to make a pounce bag. Dust the inside edge of the flesh hoop where it will make contact with the shell to keep the wet skin

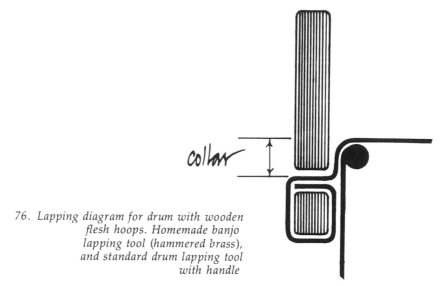

76. *Lapping diagram for drum with wooden flesh hoops. Homemade banjo lapping tool (hammered brass), and standard drum lapping tool with handle*

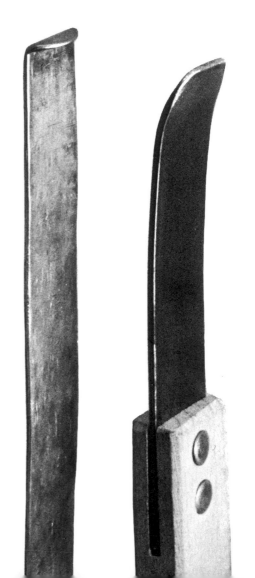

from sticking to the shell. Place the hoop on the shell and lap the other flesh hoop.

When the second hoop has been lapped and has set enough to be placed on the shell, spread a clean, dry towel on the table and invert the shell with the head down on the towel. Dust the second head and place it on the shell with a weighted board on top. The weight will keep the hoops from popping off if hoop warp is extreme. Leave in a cool, dry place where drying can occur slowly. When thoroughly dry, normally nine or ten hours, the hoops will probably have warped somewhat.

Sponge both heads on both sides until they come back into position. Place them back on the shell, position the counter hoops and rope up the drum. (See Drum Mounting, page 72). Tension the drum sufficiently to pull the counter hoops down below the rim of the shell. Tension one rope and then the rope diametrically opposite to ensure that the hoops remain level. Allow to dry thoroughly.

Release the tension and take as much slack out of the rope as you can by surging the rope (feeding it forward) from beginning to end. If you have drum grips, they will assist in this operation. After all the slack is out and the rope tied off, the drum is ready to play. When not being played, rope-tensioned drums—unlike rod-tensioned drums—are slacked off to keep the rope from stretching.

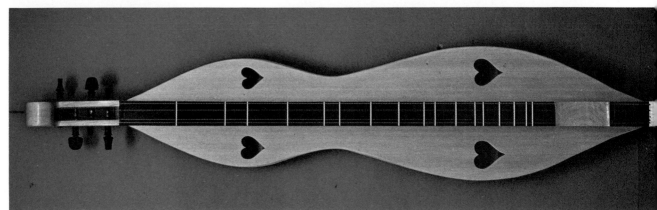

Instruments designed and built by Irving Sloane

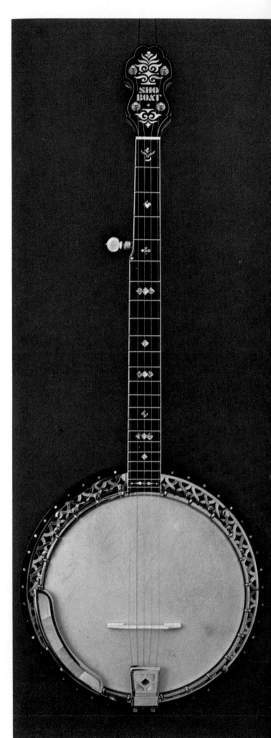

Alto recorder built by
Arnold Dolmetsch Ltd.

Braces and Ropes

Leather braces (also called buffs, tugs, pulls, ears) must be made strong enough to withstand severe strain. Tab-type braces, such as those on the old Potter drums, used a semisoft grade of leather ranging in thickness from $1/8''$ to $3/16''$ with a sueded nap on both sides to take white polish. The white tab braces on my Fife drum were purchased from Potter's after many abortive attempts to bleach leather white, a process seemingly beyond amateur possibility.

For the Belgian drum I used a saddle-grade leather $1/8''$ thick. On this kind of tapered sleeve brace, the holes are made with an awl; tab brace holes are cut with a leather punch. Lacing is done with rawhide strips saved from the trimmings of drum skins. The strips are soaked in cold water for five minutes before lacing so that they will shrink tight. No matter what brace you use, cut a thin metal pattern of the blank shape so that all braces will be cut uniformly.

The most desirable attribute a drum rope can have is minimal stretch or elasticity. If the rope stretches easily it will require a continual, laborious retightening to remove all slack so that the braces can do their job properly. In the past, ropes of four-, five-, and seven-strand hemp were produced for drum makers. The last Belgian *cordier* making seven-strand drum rope closed shop in 1975. For the Fife drum I used a fine grade of four-strand Italian hemp rope, bought from Potter's. The standard rope diameter for snare drums is 6 mm and a guard-pattern snare drum takes about thirty-five feet of rope. This figure varies depending on the number of hoop holes. Some varieties of synthetic rope sold by yachting supplies dealers will work if they are not of the glossy hard nylon type that affords a poor gripping surface for leather braces, and if stretching is minimal.

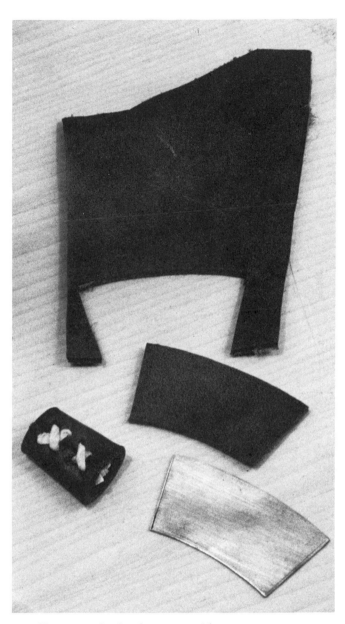

77. *Sleeve type leather brace cut with metal template, laced with calfskin trimmings and knotted off inside*

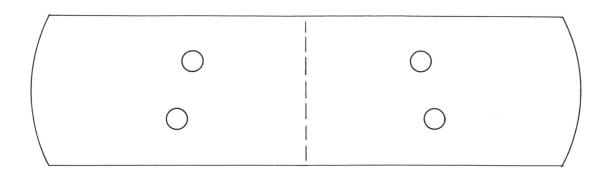

78. Template and knotless lacing pattern
for tab type braces using $^5/_{16}''$
wide calfskin (rawhide) lacing strip

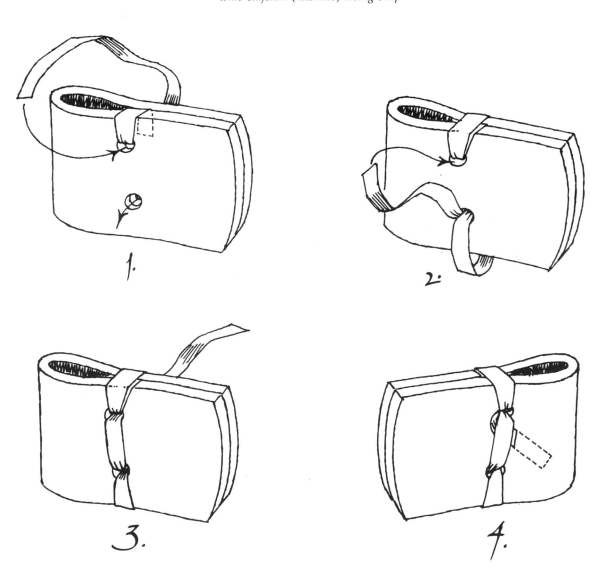

1.

2.

3.

4.

Rope Slides

Metal rope slides are more decorative than utilitarian on laminate hoops because cross-banded lamination makes rope grooving less likely than on a hoop bent of solid wood. Slides do protect the paint and also add some dazzle that fits right in with the flamboyant character of the regimental snare drum.

Trace the pattern in Fig. 79 and transfer the drawing to a sheet of twenty-six-gauge (.016") brass. Cut out as many blanks as you need with jeweler's snips or a good pair of scissors. Drill the two holes in each blank and file smooth the blank contour. The counter hoop made to be cut up into flesh hoops is used as a jig for shaping the slides.

Clamp the hoop flat on the workbench with one edge protruding a few inches out from the bench. Clamp by laying a board across the hoop parallel to the bench edge and clamp on both ends. The hoop must be immobilized with clear access to about a six-inch portion of the hoop.

Drive a small brad into the center of the hoop section standing clear. Position the brad ³/8" from the top edge and hammer it in angled downwards.

Clip off all but about ³/32" of the brad. Place the pointed portion of the blank on the brad and firmly press the blank over the top of the hoop to fix the two bends. Hold it in place and hammer it to conform to the curve of the hoop. Use a plastic-headed hammer with a slightly domed face to avoid marking the blank. Remove the slide and place it top down on a thick piece of leather. Hammer two ball-shaped depressions in the flat section of the slide with a dapping punch that has a ¹/4" ball. If you grind a rounded end onto a piece of metal rod or bolt, it will do the same job. One hammer blow is enough for each depression and this will distort the blank somewhat. Put it back on the hoop and hammer it back into conformity. The dip between the two brass blisters can be accentuated by laying a round bar across the valley between them and giving it a tap. Polish on a buffing wheel with rouge.

Before installing the slides, make sure they are positioned correctly along the lie of the rope. Affix with two small brads after making guide holes with a brad awl.

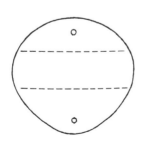

79. Pattern for rope slides and raising two bumps with ball end dapping tool over leather pad

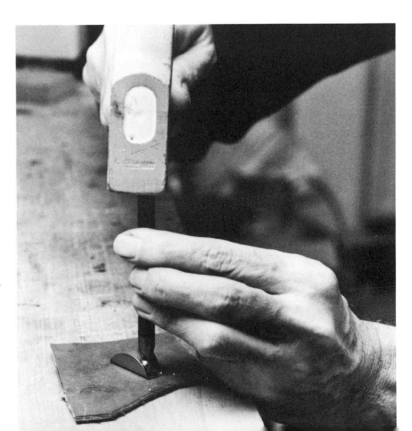

80. Cadet size snare drum (author's design and construction):

Brass shell: 13¹/₂" x 10"
Hoops: 14³/₈" x 1⁹/₁₆" x ³/₈", ten holes
Snare: Six strand gut

Decoration

Counter hoops can be left natural, or can be stained or painted. Traditional designs for British military drums used heraldic devices with regimental colors used on the shell, hoop borders, and wavy stripe called the worm. European drums also employed heraldic designs but hoop design favored triangles and stripes. Nineteenth-century American drums used Federal motifs showing eagles and shields while hoops were left unadorned or painted a solid color. Late nineteenth-century drums occasionally display hoops bearing repeat black filigree patterns on the natural wood.

On the Belgian drum I gilded the alternating silver and gold triangles on a dark blue ground. The hoops were first coated with a flat white prime-sealer. Primers can be tinted to match the top coat but a white undercoat improves the luminosity of primary colors. Two coats of blue polyurethane paint bought from a boat supply shop were then applied. This finish was smoothed with a light sanding, and two coats of clear polyurethane varnish were applied. When thoroughly dry, the surface was carefully smoothed with #600 grit wet-or-dry paper.

The triangles were laid out on the hoops with dividers, their pointed legs pressed in to leave marks. Lines connecting the marks were drawn with a sharp pencil to define the triangles. A clear bronzing liquid, books of aluminum and gold leaf, and a gilder's tip were bought at an art supply shop.

81. *Gilding equipment: Book of gold leaf, gilder's tip, and soft haired brush for pressing down leaf and sweeping off surplus.*

Leaf is also available in a cheaper false gold. I prefer leaf to paint because of its metallic brilliance and smoothness, qualities that cannot be had with metallic paints.

The bronzing liquid was carefully painted in the triangles with a small artist's brush, and left for forty-five minutes to acquire the proper degree of tack. Working from the back of the book, each leaf was sliced with a single-edge razor and lifted onto the sized area with the gilder's tip. The tip is first brushed over one's face to pick up a trace of skin oil so the leaf will cling to the tip. Gilders sometimes massage a tiny dab of Vaseline into their inner left wrist to help matters. The leaf is delicately pressed down into the size with a soft-haired varnish brush, also used to sweep away surplus bits of leaf.

Gilding must be done in a room free of air currents that might flutter the leaf into an unmanageable jumble. It can be an exasperating process until you get the knack but is an important technique for decorative use.

Tack time varies for bronzing liquids, and the manufacturer's directions should be followed. The final gilding of the hoops was given twenty-four hours to dry thoroughly and the surface was then lightly polished with a clean piece of cotton flannel. A finish coat of clear polyurethane varnish was applied.

For the Fife drum shell, I cut letters out of fourteen-gauge brass sheet with a jeweler's saw. They

82. Letters cut from 14 gauge sheet brass with jeweler's saw

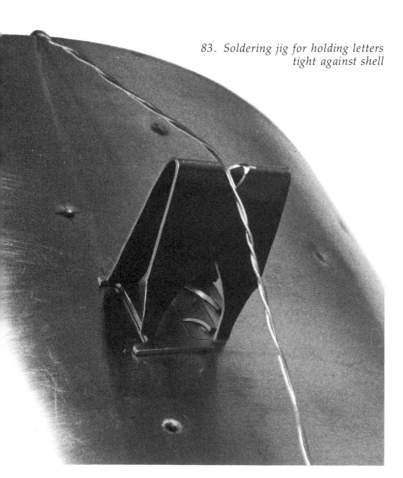

*83. Soldering jig for holding letters
tight against shell*

were bent to conform to shell curvature and held in place for soft-soldering with a folded metal prop wedged under a wire stretched around the shell wall (83).

The positions for the $^5/_{16}$" diameter stainless steel balls were laid out on the shell and each place was marked with a small depression made by a single hammer blow on a ball-end dapping tool. Hammering was done with the shell supported on a rounded two-by-four clamped to the workbench. Without support you risk deforming a large area while making a small dot. The dot is just to keep the balls from rolling off while being soldered. Cut soft silver soldering wire into small pieces and set a piece next to the ball with tweezers. Drop some flux on the soldering area and heat the ball with a fine burner tip. If the solder does not flow into the joint under the ball, it can only be because the joint was not thoroughly cleansed with fine emery paper. The ball, too, must be clean at the soldering juncture to make a solid joint.

The shell itself was then sanded with emery paper and then scrubbed in a tub of hot water and detergent to clean off all soil, traces of dried flux, and fingerprints. All the soldering joints were then carefully checked to make sure they were securely

84. *Repoussé brass shell (tenor drum)*
using flat strip reinforcing
around edges
(National Army Museum, London)

soldered. The surface was primed with a matte red primer over which were painted two coats of red enamel; the paints were formulated for use on metal. When thoroughly dry, rough spots were smoothed away with water and #400 grit wet-or-dry sandpaper. A week later I applied a clear coat of polyurethane varnish over the entire face of the shell, letters and balls included.

Repoussé, the raising of embossed designs on a metal surface, is an ancient technique that has often been used on drums in the past. A design is traced in reverse on the inside of the joined shell. The outline is then hammered into relief with a chasing tool. Sculptural effects are achieved by hammering out the design from the inside of the shell with the shell resting on a thick piece of leather or fastened to a bed of chaser's pitch. As work progresses, hammered areas must be occasionally annealed to soften them as they become work hardened. A complete description of repoussé technique appears in *Metal Techniques for Craftsmen* by Oppi Untracht.

85. *American militia artillery snare drum, 1815. Red painted shell and hoops with multi-color decoration (Guthman Collection)*

86. *Drum grip made from rubber pulley belt, hooks covered with plastic tubing to protect hoop finish*

Drum Mounting

Drum assembly is greatly facilitated by the use of drum grips—rods that grip both hoops and exert enough clamping pressure to immobilize the hoops while they are being roped. Three are normally used for mounting a drum. I use three heavy rubber rings with padded S-hooks as makeshift grips and they do a fair job of holding the hoops in place. They are stretched very tight when applied, which means another person's help is required to get them on.

Begin by splicing a small loop in one end of the rope. A loop can also be made by whipping the end to the rope with heavy-duty thread. Whip the other end and dip it in white glue or shellac to prevent the tip from fraying.

When all the holes are roped, pull out as much slack as possible and tie off at the beginning loop. With the braces up against the top flesh hoop, surge the line again from beginning to end to remove any remaining slack. Additional tension can be gained by working the rope through the bottom of the roping all around the shell.

Roping can be finished off decoratively by knotting surplus rope in the style of a drag rope. This is simply a slip knot with a loop repeatedly brought through a loop. Drag ropes were originally used as a sling to enable the drummer to carry his drum on his back. Gradually, they have evolved into a purely decorative device popular with all drum corps.

87. Three grips anchor hoops
while roping

88. Traditional metal
rod grips, jaws
lined with felt
or rubber

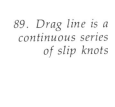

89. Drag line is a
continuous series
of slip knots

73

Tambourine

Known among diverse cultures in many parts of the world, the tambourine is one of the oldest percussive instruments and has come down to us in its original form; it looks today as it appears in ancient relief carvings and paintings. Essentially a shallow-frame drum, it consists of a wooden shell with single skin head glued or nailed on. The shell is slotted to hold small pairs of metal discs called jingles that vibrate when the head is struck or the tambourine shaken.

Traveling minstrel shows popularized the tambourine during the late nineteenth century, and it became a familiar fixture of Salvation Army street bands, doing double duty as rhythmic accompaniment and collection box. The flashing motion, metallic rustle, and percussive thump of tambourines have a tantalizing, crowd-rousing effect that has made them an important part of religious revival and gospel music in America.

Tambourines are a traditional instrument in Middle Eastern music and during the eighteenth century they were introduced into what became known as the janissary section of English military bands. Late in that century the tambourine achieved a vogue in England as a genteel diversion for well-bred ladies, who danced as they played. Tambourines were also used as accompaniment for the piano and much music was published around 1800 for tambourine and piano duo employing sophisticated notation for tambourine consistent with highly refined playing techniques. Novel percussive and rhythmic techniques included *flamps, travales, jingles, bass,* and *turn.*

Despite evidence of virtuoso tambourine skills, the tambourine faded away as a parlor fad, leaving no discernible impress on the serious music establishment. Not until the late nineteenth century did the tambourine emerge as a special effects instrument in the symphony orchestra.

91. *Tambourine shell
with finished cutouts and
interior hand grip*

Tambourine Shells

Tambourine shells are normally between ten and eleven inches in diameter and contain six double slots holding twelve pairs of jingles. Modern shells often have the slots staggered, but I prefer the traditional tandem arrangement because of the larger area left for decoration between slot groupings.

The shell should be made of nine laminations, which is strong enough to withstand the pounding that tambourines receive and considerably stronger than commercially made tambourines. Shell depth is $2^1/4''$ with jingles of $1^7/8''$ diameter.

Prepare a shell. (See Laminate Shells and Hoops, page 13.) Make a sketch of the side view of the shell including two slot groupings plus whatever design you wish to use. Find the slot spacing by dividing the circumference by seven. Mark this dimension on the edge of a piece of paper and lay it on the shell. Mark off seven spaces, the eighth line, hopefully, falling right on your first one. Pencil these lines across the face of the shell with a try square. Each line represents the center of a slot grouping except for one, which is left intact for a hand hold.

Carefully pencil in all the slots, leaving a separating strip between slots of not less than $7/32''$ thickness. Numerous slot possibilities exist, the simplest being to drill a hole the size of the slot at each end and saw out the waste piece with an adjustable coping saw. The slot length should be $2\frac{1}{4}''$, longer if the ends are oval; enough room must be allowed to permit free rattling of the jingles. The depth of the slot should be twice the central thickness of a pair of jingles and not less than $7/16''$.

Cut out oval-ended or other unusual slot shapes by drilling a small hole in each slot to accept the blade of an adjustable coping saw. I found that the best way of sawing slots was to clamp the shell flat on the workbench with the sawing area jutting out from the edge. Clamp by positioning a board across the top of the shell, clamped to the workbench at each end. This arrangement holds the shell rigid while sawing is done with the saw blade positioned horizontally, the frame standing upright. If you are using the large-hole-on-each-end arrangement, clamp a wooden caul under the hole to be drilled to prevent fracturing the inner face veneer as the drill exits.

I like to line the bottom edge of a shell with ebony or other hard material—rosewood, ivory, plastic are all possibilities. A lining offers protection and decoration and should be added before cutting the slots. It can be omitted.

The ebony lining was cut from a discarded guitar fretboard. First the board was smoothed on both sides with a scraper blade. The inner and outer shell contour was then traced onto the ebony. The outside contour was cut out and the board was clamped in a vise. A backsaw was used to cut through the

center of the $1/4''$ thickness so that the cutting of the inside contour of the shell freed two $1/8''$ strips.

Each strip was glued to the edge with epoxy and clamped overnight. Strips are fitted together with an oblique joint to provide a larger gluing surface and the last piece is cut to gently wedge in place (93). Four strips were required to line the edge. The edges were finished flush with the shell using file, scraper blade, and sandpaper. On shells that have an edge lining, the shell depth is sized to include the lining in the $2\frac{1}{4}''$ depth.

On the rosewood-faced shell I incorporated a decorative white line to separate the dark ebony lining from the dark rosewood shell. This was done by simply gluing a layer of maple veneer to each side of the ebony board before cutting out the lining.

Tambourines usually have a thumb hole in the shell, but most players wrap their hand around the shell with their middle finger through the hole from the inside. A more practical kind of grip is a small shelf glued to the inner face of the shell. This shelf provides a comfortable hand grip with the thumb around the outside resting on the top edge. I have experimented with various positions for the shelf and a central placement seems the most natural one, but my hand is large and the shelf might be made more convenient for a smaller hand by shifting it toward the bottom or making it smaller.

Trace the inner contour of the shell on a $1/4'' \times 1\frac{1}{4}'' \times 5''$ piece of ebony, maple, or other hardwood and saw out the shelf. Tape or rubber-cement a piece of medium-grit sandpaper to the inner face of the shell and rub the gluing edge of the shelf back and forth until it makes a tight joint with the curved surface. Glue with epoxy and clamp overnight.

92. Shell using brass brads as design element

93. Edge lining of
ebony and maple veneer
sandwich, each
piece cut to wedge
into gluing position

94. *Slightly dome faced hammer locked in vise serves as anvil for hammering jingles*

Jingles

Tambourine jingles can be worked to emit sounds ranging from a bright, bell-like jingling to the dark, rustling sound favored by many professional percussionists. The hardness, thickness, and density of the metal used plus the shape of the jingle are all important factors in determining the quality of the sound. Thicker jingles, such as the cast-bronze jingles used in the Middle East, tend toward a bell tone. Thinner jingles are lower in pitch but hardening a jingle through hammering raises its pitch and will take it progressively from a dull sound to a jingling tone as doming occurs.

I have experimented with three alloys in making jingles—brass, nickel silver, and phosphorus bronze. All were purchased in twenty-two-gauge (.025″) cut from rolls. Since all had to be hammered, it made sense to start off with a soft or medium-hard metal. Where the gauge metal I wanted was available only in a hard grade, I softened it by annealing.

Brass, the most important of the copper alloys, consists basically of various proportions of copper and zinc, the standard for yellow brass being about 65% copper to 35% zinc. Nickel silver, known also as German silver or new silver, is an alloy of copper, zinc, nickel, and a trace of manganese. There is no silver in it and formulations are designated by their percentage of nickel content, such as the 18% nickel silver I used for my jingles. Phosphorus bronze is a copper and tin alloy with a small amount of phosphorus added. It is a tough, resilient metal with superior resistance to corrosion, slightly heavier than nickel silver. Nickel silver also has high tarnish resistance and is more dense than brass, which does tarnish.

I chose these metals because of their different

compositions and densities and the interesting color range they offer—brass, silver, and copper. The flat discs were cut from the sheet with a circle cutter in a drill press. The radius was set at $^{15}/_{16}$" to cut blanks of $1^{7}/_{8}$" diameter, a good size for a ten-inch shell. Set the center drill in the cutter at a level where it makes a hole before the cutter makes contact. Clamp the metal to a board so that it is immobilized close to the circle being cut. After each disc is cut, unclamp, move the metal along and clamp again. Discs can also be cut out with tin snips or a jeweler's saw, but this takes much longer to do.

Jingles are domed by carving a shallow depression in a hardwood block. The center of the depression need not be more than $^{1}/_{8}$" deep. A small brad nailed into the center of the depression will center the jingle for hammering. The width of the depression depends on whether you want a hatlike jingle with a rim or one that is convex from edge to edge.

Jingles that are too hard to hammer must be annealed. Place them on a charcoal block and heat them with a brisk flame from a medium-size burner tip for about ten seconds. They do not have to get red hot to be annealed; a brief amount of heating will soften them to the point where they can be easily domed. Use a round-faced hammer to punch in the jingles on the doming block. I use the same hammer locked in a vise as an anvil for hammering the jingles to the right degree of hardness. Hammering is done best with a jeweler's chasing hammer but any slightly domed hammer will do.

As doming and hammering progress, slip the jingles onto a loose-fitting metal spindle or nail and listen to their sound by striking them and rattling pairs. In this way, you can decide which sound you like best.

On all the jingles, I beveled both sides of the edge with a flat file. This lowers the pitch even though the bevel is only about $^{1}/_{32}$" wide. I beveled the brass jingles to a greater degree, introducing a gradual taper from about $^{1}/_{4}$" in from the edge. This gave the tone a cymballike quality with a slower decay. Everything I did—hammering just around the hole, hammering just the edge area, hammering to a greater or lesser degree of hardness—affected the tone in some way. No attempt was made to tune the jingles—a poor idea, I think—or to smooth out the rough patina of hammering, an attractive hallmark of a handmade jingle.

Of the three tambourines, the hat-shaped nickel-silver jingles gave the tone I liked best. The convexly domed phosphorus-bronze jingles produced a darker, more clattering sound and the brass jingles—convex with a slight flattening of the edge—had a more shimmering, sibilant sound.

95. Cutting jingles with circle cutter in drill press

Installing Posts and Jingles

From the top edge drill a ⅛″ hole down through the center of each slot grouping. Drill ⅛″ past the bottom edge of the lower slots. This job can be done accurately and quickly on a drill press or a good portable drill mounted in a vertical drill stand.

Cut as many ⅛″ diameter brass posts as you need to a size that is ¼″ longer than the total height of a slot grouping. This should give you a buried surplus of ⅛″ on each end. Dab some epoxy into the holes at the bottom of the lower slots. Push the posts in, threading on the jingles in each slot. Use a piece of ⅛″ brass rod in the top hole to ram down the posts when they get below the rim. Make sure the posts are all seated in the bottom holes.

Buy some ⅛″ hardwood doweling and cut off slightly oversize pieces to fill the post holes. Daub some epoxy on each dowel before inserting them. Tap them in as far as they will go with a small hammer. Leave overnight to dry and then saw off the protruding dowels and file them flush. Posts installed in this manner have a good chance of staying in place until the tambourine falls apart.

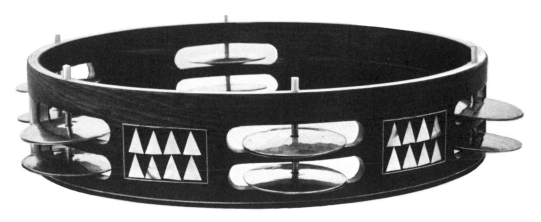

96. Dowels gluing in post holes

Installing Head

A ten-inch tambourine shell needs a skin 3″ larger, giving a margin of 1½″ all around. Goatskin heads are sometimes used but calfskin is standard on good tambourines.

Tambourines are traditionally prey to two basic ills—the posts working loose from the shell and the skin coming loose. A loose skin has to be replaced because there is not enough skin to work with on a trimmed head.

In the Middle East, tambourine skins are often glued without tacking. In the West, unless the tambourine is rod-tensioned, heads are normally fastened with tacks. And on well-made tambourines they are both glued and tacked. I have worked out two basic methods for installing heads.

Begin by wrapping a strip of ½″ plastic tape

97. *Leather lined tacking support and tacked shell*

around the shell ½" below the top edge. Keep it parallel to the rim by using a ½" strip of cardboard as a gauge. If there is any finish in this gluing area, scrape it off down to the bare wood with a single-edge razor blade or sandpaper. Also scrape bare the top edge.

Prepare a tacking support (97) and have handy six 4" rubber bands at least ¼" wide. Also prepare two discs slightly larger than your shell. Use ¾" plywood or pressed wood. Accuracy in cutting out the discs is unimportant. On one of the discs, draw a circle ¾" in from the edge. Cut out on this line and glue a thin facing of rubber on one side of this ring.

Submerge the skin in cold water—never hot—for five minutes. Remove the skin and towel off surplus moisture. Skins can be mounted smooth side up or rough side up, the latter preferred by percussionists because the roughness helps the thumb roll.

Brush liquid hide glue on the top edge and the scraped side area of the shell. Place the shell on the hammering support, center the skin, and drive in a tack ¼" from the top edge. Move to the diametrically opposite side, pull the skin taut without actu-

ally stretching it, and drive in a second tack. Use a tack with a large head that will bite the skin and hold it without cutting into it. Move around the rim, alternating opposite sides and keeping the skin taut. Use at least fourteen tacks for a ten-inch tambourine.

Pull the rubber bands over the tacked edge to press the skin into good contact with the glue-coated surface. Smooth out wrinkles in the side.

Place the clamping ring on top of the shell, rubber face down. Position the solid disc under the shell and apply at least six clamps (98). Leave overnight under pressure. The next day, remove the clamps and rubber bands and slice off the surplus skin. Use a razor blade or very sharp knife and follow the ridge of the plastic tape underneath the skin. Save all skin scraps.

Clip off the protruding ends of the tacks inside the shell with an end-cutting nipper. File away any vestige of the tacks with a pad-end riffler file. Leave nothing that might snag fingers.

An alternate method I have experimented with relies heavily on a strong glue joint.

Apply the tape and scrape off any finish as be-

82

98. Gluing jig to ensure effective glue joint between skin and rim

sary—tied right up against the inside shell. After they shrink tight and hard, clip off the ends.

The advantage of the clamping-with-discs system is that the side area and the top become two separate zones of shrinkage, and gluing the top edge becomes a practical possibility. Without the tightly clamped ring, head shrinkage would draw the glue line away from the edge toward the center; the continual movement of the skin while shrinking would render that glue joint ineffectual. This overall shrinkage would also draw up the side skin area much more than it does with the clamp arrangement. Movement of the side skin area can be further controlled by coating this area with varnish after the skin has thoroughly dried.

99. Slicing away surplus skin with razor blade

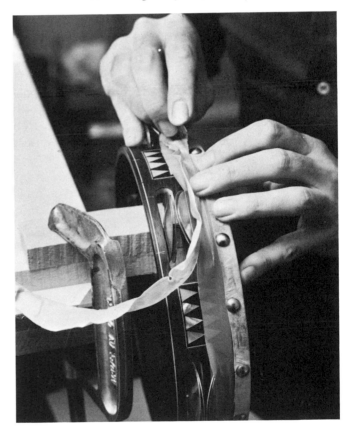

fore. Drill fourteen pairs of $1/16''$ holes spaced $1/4''$ apart and $1/4''$ below the rim. Soak the skin and apply glue to the gluing area on the shell as before. Place the shell on a flat surface and center the skin on the shell. Put on a rubber band and pull the skin taut. Put on the other rubber bands, keeping the head taut. Apply the discs top and bottom and clamp as before. Dry overnight or a minimum of ten hours in a cool dry place.

Remove the clamps and rubber bands and trim off the surplus skin. Using a sharp-pointed awl, carefully poke through each of the drilled holes. Puncture the skin and twist the awl as it goes into the hole. Make the skin hole the same size as the drilled hole by twisting the awl and not by ramming it in and out. Withdraw it carefully so that it does not pull the skin hard enough to break the glue joint.

Cut fourteen strips of lacing from the surplus skin, each one measuring $3''$ long and $3/16''$ wide in the middle. Taper the ends to a point. Soak them in cold water for five minutes and towel them off. Thread them through each pair of holes and make one overhand knot—a full square knot is unneces-

100. Ten inch rosewood veneered shell, twenty phosphorus bronze jingles

Decoration

Tambourines can be attractively decorated with designs applied with paints, inks, metallic leaf, inlay, and small brads. I have avoided the overall use of painted backgrounds, preferring the chip-free safety of colored stains. Paint poses a problem especially where slot edges come in contact with jingles. Design elements can be painted on the shell surface without fear of chipping or rubbing off if two or three finish coats of clear polyurethane varnish are used to seal the designs.

On one tambourine (92) I used a design painted on the natural surface with India ink. Certain elements in the design are accentuated by the use of small brass brads, which lend bright textural interest to the black design.

The shell was first smoothed with fine garnet paper, and a wash coat of shellac (1 part white shellac to 5 parts alcohol) was applied to the entire shell except the ebony hand grip; a smooth piece of ebony has a nice feel that is lost by coating it with a finish. Unless the shell itself is wash coated, India ink will fuzz or bleed into the wood grain.

The design was carefully drawn on a piece of tracing paper, the back blacked with a soft pencil, and then taped in position on the shell. After the designs were traced onto the shell with a sharp pencil, they were painted in with an artist's #1 sable brush and waterproof India ink. Each round dot in the design marked the place for a roundhead brass brad.

A short length of two-by-four was clamped to the workbench with four inches protruding over the edge. This end was rounded with a rasp file to match the inner contour of the shell. Starter holes were made with a sharp-pointed awl, each brad was held in pace with a tweezer and hammered in. All hammering was done with the shell positioned on the two-by-four support. Protruding ends of the brads inside the shell were clipped off and filed flush with a pad-end riffler, leaving no rough edges to snag fingers.

Interesting variations of this style of decoration can be achieved by using colored inks, or making a design entirely of brads on a dark-stained background. Mask off the top 1/2" of the shell with masking tape, and coat all designs with two, preferably three, coats of clear polyurethane varnish. Apply light, even coats carefully brushed on to avoid runs or drips. On designs using brads, it is best not to do

84

any final polishing. If the varnish is polished off the brads, they will tarnish.

On the tambourine with the speckled-stain finish I inlaid 3 mm pearl dots spaced 3/4" apart in the bottom ebony lining. Same-size holes were drilled and the dots set in with epoxy. They were set in protruding slightly above the surface and were filed flush afterwards.

The entire shell was sanded very smooth with fine garnet paper. The shell was tinted with a pale green alcohol stain applied with a clean rag, and then spattered with a small random pattern of black speckles. A discarded toothbrush was dipped in India ink and sprayed on the shell by rubbing a thumb over the bristles.

The design was transferred with tracing paper, the top 1/2" of the shell masked off, and two coats of clear polyurethane varnish applied. The design was clearly visible through the varnish, which was lightly smoothed with #600 wet-or-dry paper to prepare the surface for gilding. Gold and aluminum leaf were applied to the design using the same method as on the drum hoops. (See page 68.) After gilding was completed, three more coats of varnish were applied and rubbed to a soft sheen with a felt pad, fine pumice, and mineral oil. Three days of drying time was allowed before rubbing. A higher finish can be obtained by polishing with Duco #7 Auto Polishing liquid briskly rubbed on with a felt pad and buffed clean with a flannel cloth.

101. Left: Ten inch maple shell, twenty-four brass jingles
Right: Ten and a half inch maple shell, twenty-four nickel-silver jingles

Appalachian Dulcimer

102. Typical dulcimer shape, sitka spruce top, birdseye maple sides and back

Fretted zithers comprise a large group of instruments that have appeared in many countries in slightly varying form. These include the Swedish *humle*, the French *épinette des Vosges*, the English hammered dulcimer, the Norwegian *langeleik*, the Dutch *hommel*, and the German *scheitholt*. All are characterized by an elongated sound box with pierced sound holes, frets, the use of drone strings, and a manner of playing in which the instrument lies flat on a table or in one's lap.

The Appalachian dulcimer evolved from this family of instruments although, like most folk instruments, its precise origin is obscure. Settlers in the Appalachian mountain regions came from England and northern Europe, and the dulcimers they played were probably homespun versions of similar instruments remembered from distant homelands.

Currently, the dulcimer is enjoying a lively renaissance with much popular interest in its history, music, and construction. Much of this has to do with its simple charm and ease of playing, but the dulcimer more than any other instrument wears an aura of nostalgia, a wistful echo of some legendary time when graciousness, sentiment, and repose gave a more secure sense of one's place in the scheme of things.

Dulcimers come in different shapes. The design I have chosen is a typical example but uses a hollow fretboard assembly instead of one with a solid base because it sounds better. This design, with some minor modifications, is based on a full-size blueprint available from Scott Antes (Suppliers, page 159).

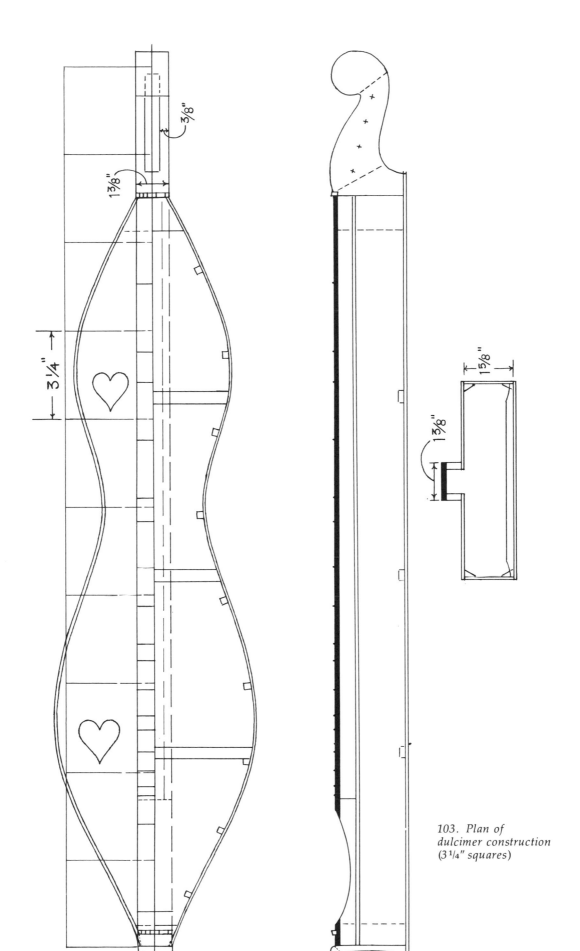

3/8"

13/8"

3 1/4"

15/8"

13/8"

103. Plan of
dulcimer construction
(3 1/4" squares)

87

Construction

All the dulcimer parts are cut to shape before assembly, which occurs in five basic steps: (1) Back cut to shape with braces and end blocks glued in; (2) Fretboard assembly with soundboard glued on; (3) Sides glued to back with peg head glued in place; (4) Fretboard/soundboard assembly glued to box; (5) End plate, nut and bridge, and tuning pegs installed.

Begin by thinning both halves of the top to $1/8''$ and the back and sides to $3/32''$. (See materials list, p. 95.) Use a smoothing plane or hand scraper for preliminary removal of wood and finish down to thickness with a broad scraper blade and sanding block. Draw the contour and heart cutouts in place on one half of the soundboard. Leave an excess margin of $1/16''$ on the contoured edge. If you plan on a slight overhang, leave an excess margin of $1/8''$. Dulcimers are made both ways, the choice being a matter of personal preference. This half cutout is the basic pattern used to make the back and both halves of the top. Cut out the shape with a jigsaw or adjustable coping saw. Drill a hole in each heart, in-

sert saw blade, and cut to shape. Smooth all contours with file and sandpaper.

Draw a center line down the back and trace the half pattern in place. Reverse the pattern and trace the other half to complete the outline of the back. Draw in the tab extensions, to which the end plate and peg box are glued, and cut out the back. Mark the positions of the cross braces and draw a line $1/16''$ (or $1/8''$) inside the contoured edge. This line denotes the exterior face of the sides and serves as a guide for gluing on the sides. Cut the three cross braces, allowing for the thickness of the sides. Glue them in place with Titebond, keeping a watchful eye for any shift when clamping. After they are glued tight, chisel out the scooped ends of the braces. Round the top edges of the braces with a small block plane and sandpaper.

Saw or file out the concave portion of the tenoned foot section of the fretboard channel or base and glue on the two long side walls. Cut the fretboard to size, allowing for a slight overhang where the concave section meets the lower end of the fretboard. Smooth both sides of the fretboard level and clamp it to the edge of the workbench. Mark off the fret slots with a try square. Saw the fret slots with

104. Full size plan of peg box

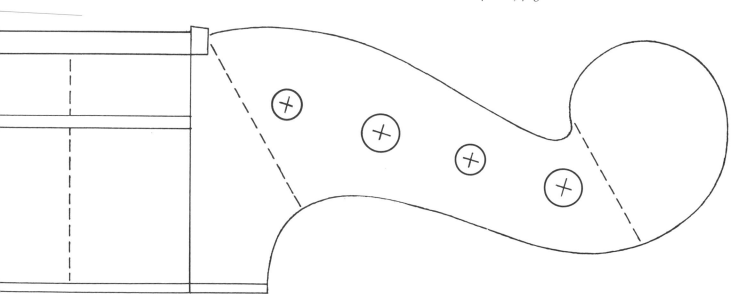

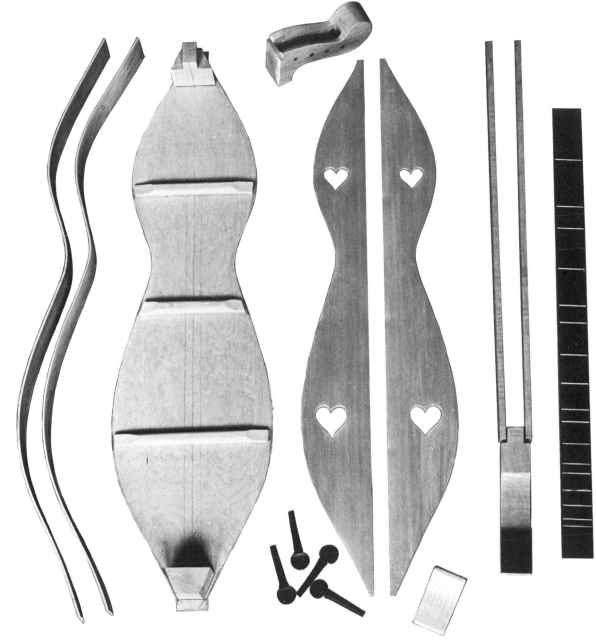

105. Dulcimer parts ready for assembly

the saw working against the edge of the try square to ensure that all the slots are parallel and straight. (See Fretboard, page 34.) If you are using a rosewood fretboard, it requires a narrower fret slot than ebony because it is softer. Normally, a larger fret wire is used on rosewood to ensure proper anchoring of the studded tang.

Glue in the small spacer block near the upper end of the base assembly. This will keep the side walls from moving out of position when the fretboard is glued on. Glue the fretboard onto the base with Titebond. Cut and glue in place the small bridge section of the fretboard, allowing for a slight overhang of the concave section. When dry, saw and file away the overhang portions of the fretboard so that the curve of the concave section makes a smooth continuity up to the top face of the fretboard. Sand smooth the outer face of the side walls

106. *Interior view of body ready for top to be glued on*

of the fretboard assembly.

Cut a ³⁄₈″ strip off the inside edge of the completed half of the soundboard. Place this trimmed half over the other half of the soundboard. Trace the outline and cut the second half to match the first. Rest both halves in place on the end blocks and set the fretboard channel assembly in place. Carefully check the fit of all parts to make sure that when they are glued they will make a tight assembly. Pencil the position of the side walls of the fretboard assembly onto the soundboard. Remove the fretboard assembly and soundboard to a flat surface and glue the fretboard base to the soundboard. When dry, reverse the entire assembly and glue in a filler piece of spruce where the bottom end of the assembly glues to the bottom block.

Bending Sides and Assembly

The bends in dulcimer sides are not extreme and can be easily accomplished without steaming or presoaking the wood. I bent the sides on a homemade bending iron (110) with an occasional moistening of the surface with a sponge. A propane torch provided heat. I found that a fine burner tip nicely balanced the heat loss from the large surface of the bending iron so that no further adjustment was necessary during bending.

Make the large waist bend first. Moisten both sides of the bending area with a sponge dipped in water. If a drop of water bounces off the heated tube, it is ready. Place the waist section on the hot tube and slowly rock it while applying gentle pressure. An area extending on both sides of the specific pressure point must be heated before bending will occur. Rocking the wooden strip helps to achieve this while preventing the scorching that might result from holding it too long in one place. Pause frequently during bending to check the sides

107. Underside view of top. Note small spacer block glued near top to stabilize fretboard assembly.

against the guideline on the back. Bend the sides so that they conform to the contour of the back and end blocks, a task not nearly as formidable as it sounds. In my dulcimer I have a gentle incurve near the bottom, a graceful touch I find pleasing. You can, however, simply leave this section straight.

If you overbend a section, you can correct it by reversing the side and pressing the bulge to the iron with mild pressure. If a crack develops during bending, continue bending with a sheet metal strip pressing against the crack to keep it from getting worse. After bending is completed, glue the crack shut with epoxy. Surface scorching can be sanded away if heat penetration is not severe enough to cause deep brown discoloration.

Prepare two of the two-part clamping jigs used to hold the sides against the end blocks while gluing. Before gluing in the sides, check the fit of the side to the back, the end blocks, and the back braces. Glue the sides one at a time. Apply Titebond or liquid hide glue to the edge of the side, the ends of the back braces, and the sides of the end blocks. Press the side into place and loosely fasten the clamping jigs. Place a thin 3″ x 24″ board over the top of the side and apply clamps. When the side looks accurately positioned against the ends of the back braces, tighten the clamping jigs. Clean up glue ooze with a damp cloth or a small artist's brush wiped clean on a damp cloth. Glue in the second side in the same manner.

Slice twenty ¼″ x ½″ x ½″ pieces from a ½″ x ½″ x 12″ spruce stick. Split the pieces diagonally with a ⅝″ chisel to form forty right angle wedges. Spot them around the glue joint between back and side and mark their position. Apply Titebond to their right angle face and bottom. Press them in place for a rub fit—clamping is unnecessary. Hold each one in place for about twenty seconds. Glue them in one by one on each side. They will strengthen the bond of side to back and also help keep the sides vertical.

Spot the remaining wedges around the top edge of both sides. Mark their position, apply glue to the long right angle side only and press in place. When all the wedges are glued tight, set the fret-

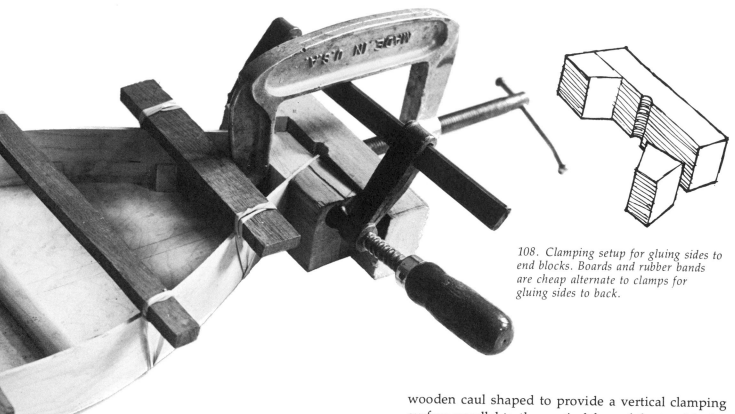

108. Clamping setup for gluing sides to end blocks. Boards and rubber bands are cheap alternate to clamps for gluing sides to back.

board/soundboard assembly in place. Check all around the sides and end blocks to make sure that the soundboard assembly will glue on with a gap-free, snug fit. When you are satisfied that all is well, remove the soundboard assembly and set it aside for the moment.

Trim the protruding ends of the sides flush with the ends of the blocks. Bandsaw the shape of the peg box out of a 1½" x 3¼" x 6" block of hardwood. Mark the position of the peg holes and drill through with a ¼" drill. Draw the peg box cutout and drill a ⅝" hole through each end. Cut out the waste portion of the peg box with adjustable coping saw or chisel. Smooth the inner surfaces with files and sandpaper wrapped around a thin block of wood. Bevel the inside top edge of the peg box, a traditional practice designed to lighten the appearance of the head.

Position the completed peg box behind the top block. Make sure it is vertically aligned with the central axis of the body. Glue the peg box in place with a clamp from the inside front face of the peg box to the front face of the top block. Make a small

wooden caul shaped to provide a vertical clamping surface parallel to the vertical face of the top block.

Before gluing on the soundboard assembly, sign your name where it can be seen through one of the heart cutouts. Apply glue to the end block shoulders, the top edge of the sides and wedges. Also apply glue to the gluing areas on the soundboard assembly. Liquid hide glue is a good choice for this job because it has a slower setting time than Titebond, allowing more time for glue application. It also permits easy separation with water and a heated knife or spatula if it ever becomes necessary to open the box.

Make an end plate of maple or other hardwood. Glue it in place with Titebond using the clamping arrangement shown in Fig. 109. Hammer in the four brass brads, leaving some of the head protruding for easy hitching of the string end loops. Drill four ¹⁄₁₆" holes where the end plate front face meets the fretboard.

Carefully measure the bridge position and define it with two shallow saw cuts. Clean out the groove with a small chisel and file. Fit the bridge and nut and glue them in place with a few dabs of glue. Both bridge and nut can be made of ebony, rosewood, maple, bone, or ivory.

Fit the pegs with a violin peg shaver and

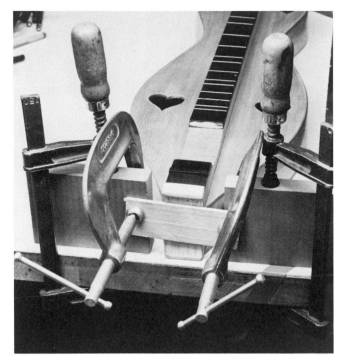

109. With peg box wedged against stop, clamping arrangement for gluing end plate

reamer. (See page 142.) If the peg taper and peg hole are perfectly round with matching tapers, the pegs will work fine. Drill a $1/16''$ hole through the center of each peg to facilitate fastening the strings.

Cut shallow grooves, just enough to grip the strings, in the nut and bridge. Five positions are shown in Fig. 103 to accommodate all stringing arrangements. String height will depend on the degree of tension you like for playing. The gap between strings and frets will be wider for lower tunings, narrower for higher tunings. A good average gap would be $3/32''$. Fix the correct height of the bridge and nut before gluing them in place.

Sand all surfaces smooth and round the edges of top and back. Finish with a sealer coat of thinned shellac (1 part shellac, 1 part alcohol) and three coats of a good oil varnish. Scuff-sand lightly between coats and allow to dry for a week before rubbing to a satin finish with #00000 or #000000 grade of steel wool.

Dulcimer strings are available in sets of varying gauges. Banjo second or thirteen-gauge strings can be used for the melody and middle strings. A wound banjo fourth or twenty-gauge string can be used for the bass string.

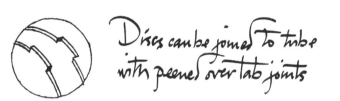

Discs can be joined to tube with peened over tab joints

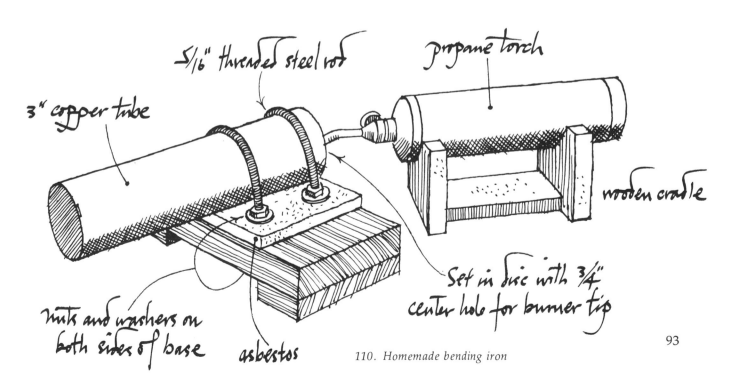

3" copper tube

5/16" threaded steel rod

propane torch

wooden cradle

Set in disc with 3/4" center hole for burner tip

nuts and washers on both sides of base

asbestos

110. Homemade bending iron

27.062″ DULCIMER FRET SCALE
(687 mm open string length)

Fret	Nut to fret inches	Nut to fret millimeters
1.	2.9497	74.922
2.	5.5779	141.679
3.	6.7825	172.276
4.	8.9929	228.420
5.	10.9624	278.445
6.	11.8651	301.374
7.	13.5215	343.446
8.	14.9974	380.934
9.	16.3125	414.338
10.	16.9152	429.646
11.	18.0213	457.741
12.	19.0067	482.770
13.	19.4584	494.243
14.	20.2873	515.297
15.	21.0258	534.055
16.	21.6838	550.769
17.	21.9854	558.429

111. Four views of completed dulcimer

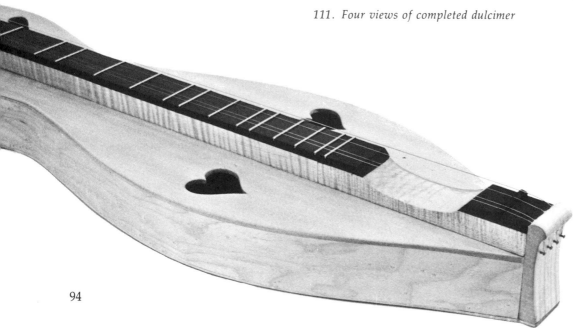

94

Dulcimer Materials List

1 back, hardwood—$^3/_{32}$" x 8$^1/_2$" x 30"

2 piece top, quartersawn spruce—@$^1/_8$" x 4" x 30"

1 peg head, hardwood—1$^1/_2$" x 3$^1/_4$" x 6"

1 spruce top block—1$^1/_4$" x 2$^1/_2$" x 2$^3/_8$"

1 spruce bottom block—1$^1/_4$" x 2$^1/_2$" x 1$^5/_8$"

3 back braces, spruce, cut from one piece—$^5/_{16}$" x $^1/_2$" x 18"

1 fretboard, rosewood or ebony—$^1/_4$" x 1$^1/_2$" x 30"

2 fretboard base sides, hardwood—@$^5/_8$" x $^5/_{16}$" x 24"

1 fretboard base foot section, hardwood—$^5/_8$" x 1$^1/_2$" x 7"

2 sides, hardwood—@ $^3/_{32}$" x 1$^5/_8$" x 30"

1 end plate, hardwood—$^3/_8$" x 1$^1/_2$" x 3"

40 gluing wedges, spruce, cut from one piece— $^1/_4$" x $^1/_2$" x 12"

30" guitar fret wire, nickel silver

4 small brass brads

4 tuning pegs, hardwood, standard violin

1 nut, rosewood or ebony—$^1/_4$" x $^5/_{16}$" x 1$^1/_2$"

1 bridge, rosewood or ebony—$^1/_4$" x $^1/_4$" x 1$^1/_2$"

Hardanger Fiddle

Violin making began its modern history in sixteenth-century Italy, a country imbued with a reverence for the artistic spirit and warmed by the golden afterglow of the Renaissance. In Brescia, Gasparo da Salo (1540–1609) was the first maker of whom anything is known, and in Cremona, a neighboring city to the south, the Amati family began the violin-making tradition brought to perfection by their famous apprentice, Antonio Stradivari (1644–1737). In Germany, violin making developed under the strong influence of Jacob Stainer (1621–1683), a superb craftsman who built models of high arching with flattened top, a style that dominated German violin making for almost a century.

Violin making began in Norway during the first half of the eighteenth century. The oldest reliably dated Hardanger fiddle (also Harding fiddle) is from the year 1750, attributed to Isak Nielsen Skaar of Hardanger. Interest in the fiddle grew quickly after 1750 and its popularity spread through the Nor-

wegian districts with which it has been historically associated. Trond Isaksen, Isak's son, was the leading maker of this period. His fiddles inspired broad imitation by other makers, who sold them at country fairs and market places.

In the nineteenth century, the Helland family of Telemark, led by Jon Erikson Helland and his two sons, Erik Johnsen Helland and Ellef Johnsen Stenkjondalen, brought an exceptional degree of flair and craftsmanship to fiddle making. After a period of study and experimentation in Copenhagen, Erik Helland brought a fresh infusion of ideas to Hardanger fiddle making, moving it closer to the mainstream of violin making. The fifty years from 1825 to 1875, encompassing the mature productions of the Helland family, comprise the finest period of Norwegian fiddle making. Ellef Johnsen, in particular, brought to his craft the eye and touch of a remarkably gifted artist. His feeling for form and ornament, and the unsurpassed elegance of his draw-

97

2. Fiddle parts on workbench (author's design and construction)

113. *Ole Jonsen Jaastad, 1651 (date doubtful),*
(Norsk Folkemuseum)

ing, place him in a class apart.

For the beginning luthier, the Hardanger fiddle is an ideal introduction to the art of violin making. If you make a Hardanger fiddle of your own design but slightly off symmetry, with marquetry somewhat imprecise, and quavery surface drawings, your fiddle will look like most of the fiddles made by Norwegian folk craftsmen. You will wind up with a charming artifact and some valuable skills gained without the perfection anxiety that goes with copying Strads.

It was in this spirit I approached the making of a Hardanger-style fiddle, my first one. The fiddle I built is a pastiche of my own and borrowed ideas from the old fiddles illustrated in this chapter.

There are many important differences between the standard violin and the Hardanger fiddle, namely: the use of sympathetic strings, no purfling, almost flat fingerboard, no linings, very small corner blocks, an overlapping f-hole, and lavish use of ornamentation and inlay. Construction techniques also differ, the most obvious being the nonuse of molds by the early Norwegian makers. The use of an integrated neck (a neck that protrudes into the body cavity supplanting the neck block) and a general lack of body symmetry attest to a moldless form

114. *Side view of fiddle by Ellef Johnsen, 1870*
(Smithsonian Collection, Sloane photo)

115. Front and back views of Ellef Johnsen fiddle (Sloane photos)

of construction used in early *lutherie* and still used by Spanish guitar makers. In this method, the neck is glued to the back of the soundboard, ensuring neck alignment from the start, and the ribs are then let into the sides of the neck heel section.

Hardanger fiddle body shapes are narrower than standard violins, with a more angular sweep of the bouts and the high arching of the German school. This tubby style of violin, markedly inferior in tone to the flatter, shallow-arched model of the Cremona masters, was apparently rooted in the simple notion that a voluptuous form would produce a voluptuous tone.

The building method I have chosen is a blend of old and new ideas designed with the novice in mind. I have stayed, for the most part, with mainstream techniques incorporating many of the changes the violin has undergone in the last one hundred fifty years.

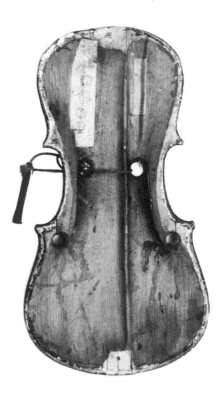

116. *Interior view of fiddle by Jon E. Helland, 1829. Bass bar integrally carved, no linings, small corner blocks (Norsk Folkemuseum).*

117. From left: Jon Erikson Helland, c. 1830;
Erik Helland, 1850. (Norsk Folkemuseum)

118. *Anonymous, c. 1900*
(Collection Haags Gemeentemuseum,
The Hague)

119. *Knudt Eriksen Helland, 1872.*
Built the year of his
death at age twenty-one
(Victoria and Albert Museum)

Construction

Building begins with the cutting of a half-pattern violin shape used to contour the mold and plates (top and back). Fig. 121 is a full-size outline of the half pattern used for my fiddle, a design you may wish to alter to suit your own preference. Cut the pattern from a thin sheet of metal and file the edges to a smooth-flowing contour. Trace both halves on a piece of paper to see how you like it as a full pat-

tern, bearing in mind that the final violin shape will be about ⅛" larger all around; the half pattern is the inner contour of the fiddle bounded by the inside face of the ribs.

The mold is cut from two ⅝" plywood boards glued together to make a mold depth of 1¼", the same depth as the ribs. Draw a dark center line on the face of the sandwich and trace the full pattern in

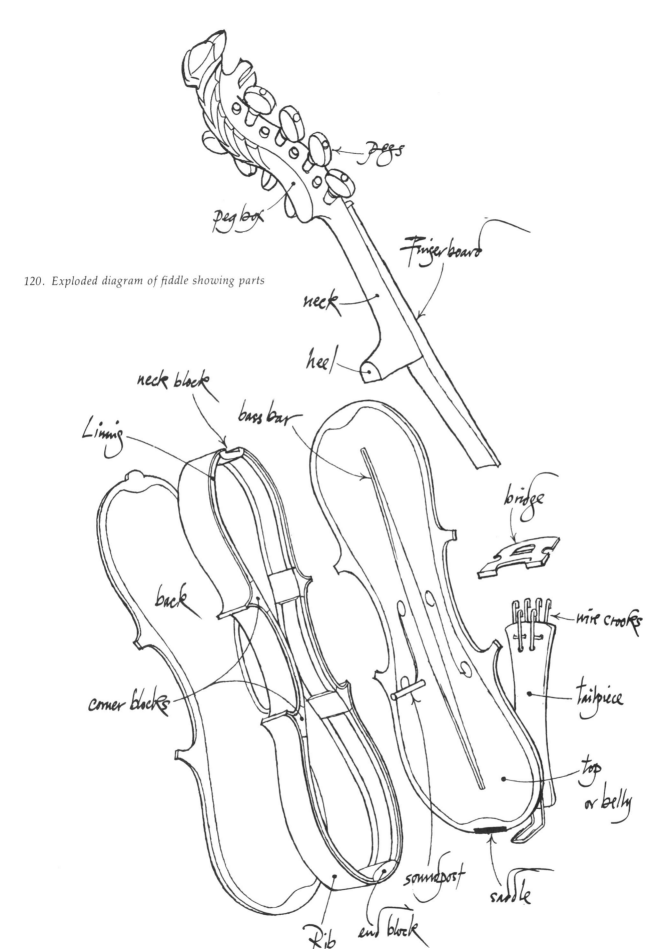

pegs

peg box

Fingerboard

120. Exploded diagram of fiddle showing parts

neck

heel

neck block

bass bar

Lining

bridge

back

wire crooks

corner blocks

tailpiece

top or belly

soundpost

saddle

Rib   end block

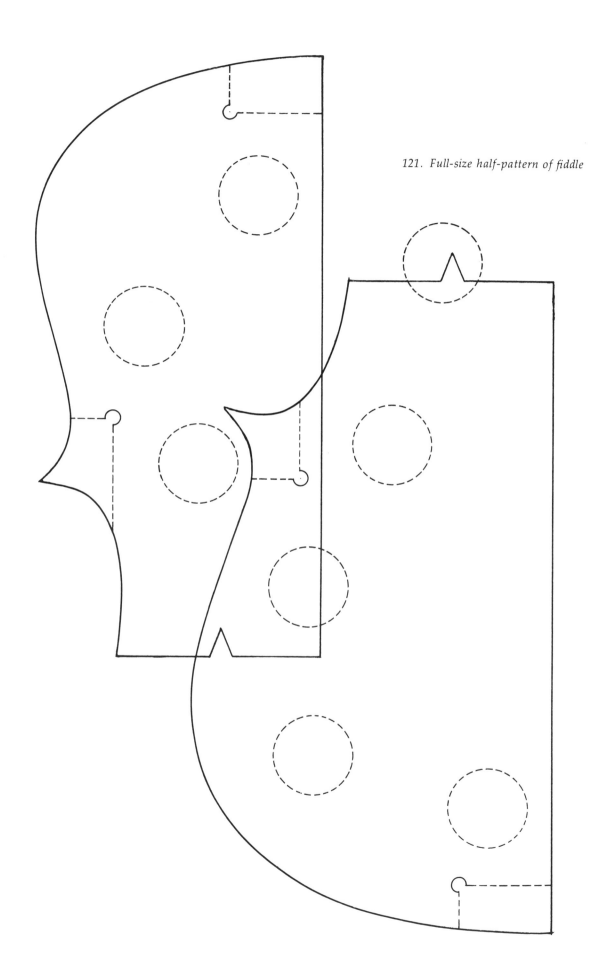

121. *Full-size half-pattern of fiddle*

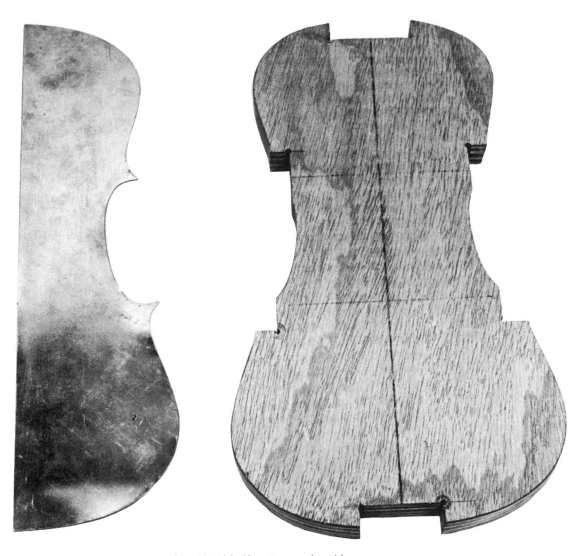

122. Metal half-pattern and mold

position. Draw in the corner block and end block cutouts, and drill hole positions. Drill the $1/8''$ corner holes and bandsaw the shape of the mold. Saw out the block cutouts and true top and sides to 90 degree accuracy. Drill the $7/8''$ clamping holes (mine are $11/16''$ because my clamps fit that size) and sand the mold smooth. The mold is now complete and can be given a protective coat of shellac or varnish.

Cut slightly oversize ($1^5/_{16}''$ deep) corner and end blocks from Sitka spruce with the grain running vertically to their top face. Glue them in place with a dab of white glue on each contact surface so that they adhere securely but can easily be severed with a thin-bladed spatula. Reposition the half pattern and trace the contour of the corners on the blocks. Saw out the corner block waste to define the corners and carefully file them to their shape, keeping them exactly vertical to the top face of the mold. Trim the end blocks and file them to a smooth, unbroken continuity with the mold.

Ribs and Linings

Ribs, or sides, are sold by dealers in violin wood as a set of three pieces; one piece forms both inner bouts, the other two pieces each provide a top and lower bout. The old Norwegian makers—whether by choice or circumstance—seem always to have used maple without figure or very subdued figure. It makes a more neutral background for surface drawings and inlay, and is cheaper to buy.

Thin the ribs to $3/64''$ with scraper blade and sandpaper fastened to a block of wood. Trim them to $1^5/_{16}''$ and cut the pieces to make the various bouts. Each piece should be longer than the bout it will encompass.

The chief hazard in bending ribs is fracturing the inner bouts because of their extreme curve. This can be neatly avoided by building a small mold to bend these inner bouts.

Cut three pieces of $1/2''$ plywood to the exact shape of the inner bout, making allowance for the thickness of a rib. Glue these three pieces to a base as shown (123) and cover with a sheet of twenty-two-gauge metal. Wrap it tightly about the form and nail it to the base on both ends. Nail a heavy strip of canvas to the bottom of the base with enough canvas to wrap completely around the form.

Boil the two ribs of the inner bouts in a covered

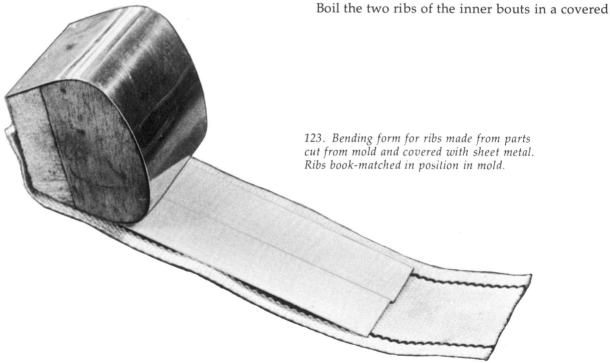

123. Bending form for ribs made from parts cut from mold and covered with sheet metal. Ribs book-matched in position in mold.

pot of water for twenty minutes. The pot should be large enough to submerge the ribs when half full. Remove the ribs with tongs and position them on the canvas so that they will be centered when they are on the form. Be sure the ribs are book-matched, and roll the form onto the wood slowly, tightly pressing the form against the wood so that no slack develops in the canvas. When completely rolled onto the form, pull over the end of the canvas strip and fasten it to the bottom of the base with push pins or tacks. Place the form in a warm 115°F. (46°C.) oven for two hours. The ribs will come off the form dry, identically formed, and permanently fixed in the precise curve of the inner bout.

A simple bending arrangement, I have found, works fine for violin making. You need a 1½″ x 10″ length of copper tubing, some ⅛″ asbestos padding, and a propane torch with fine burner tip. Clamp the tube in a vise between protective asbestos pads, and make a cradle for the torch that will focus the tip into the tube. Have handy a sponge and a bowl of water. Soak the ribs in hot water for twenty minutes.

When a drop of water sizzles off the tube, it is ready. Bend the small corner curve of each bout first. Place the end against the hot tube and use a

124. Mold with corner blocks glued in place.

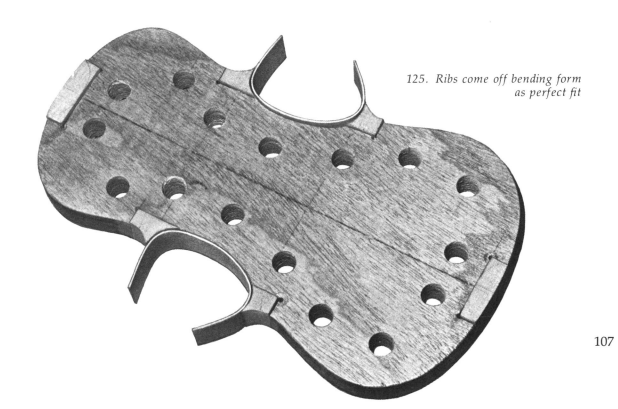

125. Ribs come off bending form as perfect fit

107

126. *Copper tube held in vise between pieces of asbestos makes simple, effective bending iron*

small block of wood held in your other hand to press the end down while the curve is taking shape on the tube. Apply steady, gentle pressure and lift the rib off periodically to check bending progress. When the corner is done, bend the large curve of the bout by rocking the wood slowly to heat a larger area than the immediate bending area. Sponge on additional water if needed and constantly check the piece against the mold to be sure it fits. Bending the upper and lower bouts is a surprisingly easy job, the ribs being as thin as they are, and assembling the rib frame will also be easy if the ribs are bent to fit well.

Fit the inner bouts to the form first. Clamp one in place with a flexible caul—heavy padding felt is perfect—that will press the rib to the mold along its entire length. Clamp the rib at the corner blocks and check the fit. Mark the edge of the corner blocks on the rib to denote the end of the gluing area. Remove the rib and pencil this line down the inside face of the rib. Smear a softened piece of soap on the mold alongside the corner blocks to keep the rib from gluing to the mold. Apply Titebond to the gluing area on the blocks and to the ends of the rib. Press in place with caul in position and apply clamps. When dry, cut off the protruding ends of the ribs to form a perfect continuity of the small curve of the upper and lower bouts where they glue to the corner blocks.

Carefully fit and glue each bout, gluing first to the corner block and then to the end blocks. The neck block will eventually be mortised for the neck so a butt joint of the upper bouts at the center juncture is unnecessary. It is important, however, for the juncture of the lower bouts at the end block to be a neatly butted joint.

After the lower bouts have been glued to the corner blocks, clamp one bout to the mold and cut it off dead center on the end block. Bring the end of the other bout around and clamp it in place. Overlap the first end on the second end and mark the joint by scoring it with a knife. Cut it off with a fine dovetail saw and both ends should now butt to a tight joint. Finish the rib frame by cutting off the overlapping ends of the ribs at the corner blocks

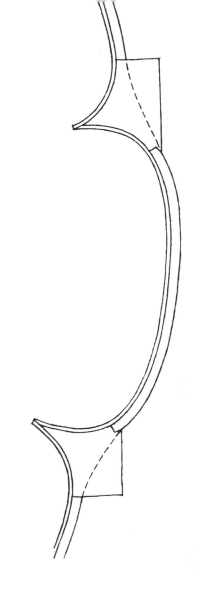

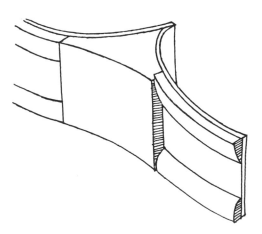

127. *Detail diagram of lining and corner blocks*

109

and file their corner juncture to a squared-off end.

The rib frame is now ready for the installation of the linings which will reinforce the rib frame and provide a larger gluing surface for the plates. Linings are cut from straight-grained spruce or willow and are ³/₃₂″ thick by about ⁵/₁₆″ wide. Boil the twelve strips as before but this time for an hour. One by one, remove them with tongs and slowly bend them to shape on the copper tube bending iron (the bending form made for the inner bout ribs will not work for the thicker linings). Bend the linings to fit each bout with an overlap at each block that will be cut off when they are fitted. If a lining cracks while bending, glue the crack shut when the linings are glued in. If possible, boil a few extra strips with the twelve to take care of any breakage.

Plane or file down the ribs and blocks flush with the mold and then sever the glue joints holding each block to the mold. Free the rib frame and slide it up on the mold to expose the area where the linings will glue. For the inner bout lining, cut a small mortise in each corner block to seat the ends. Install the linings with their top edge protruding slightly above the rib edge to preclude all possibility of their gluing below the rib edge. Glue with Titebond and clamp with rubber band-reinforced spring clothespins. The ends of the upper and lower bouts need only butt against the blocks.

When the linings are all in on this side of the rib frame, remove it from the mold. It will probably spring in a bit. Lay a thin slat about 1¹/₂″ wide on the mold across the waist. Trace the contour of the inner bouts onto the slat and cut it out. This is inserted into the rib frame between the inner bouts to act as a prop. With the prop in place install the linings on the other side. Before gluing each lining strip in, clamp it in place and check with a small try square to make sure the ribs stay at a right angle to the plane of the top. If the ribs stray out of vertical alignment, they will throw off the symmetry of the fiddle.

When the linings are all installed, carve them to their rounded taper without narrowing the top gluing edge. Cut off the surplus portions of the blocks and file them to a smooth continuity with the linings (129). Sand smooth all parts of the rib frame with fine garnet paper but stay away from the top lining edge. When all is smooth, file the lining down flush with the ribs, making sure to keep them uniformly level. The rib frame is now complete.

Drill a ¹/₄″ hole in the center of the bottom joint for the endpin. Use a caul on the face of the end block to prevent fracture of the surface when the drill exits.

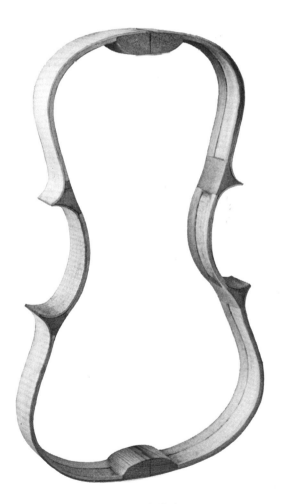

129. Completed rib frame

130. Wedge shaped gluing jig for jointing plates

Top and Back

Violin tops are cut from quartersawn spruce, the most important variety being Norway spruce (*Picea excelsa*) grown in the mountainous regions of Austria, Czechoslovakia, Rumania, and Yugoslavia. Sitka spruce (*Picea sitchensis*) is a good alternative if it is well seasoned and not too soft. Wood for making stringed instruments should be seasoned for at least two years before using. It is worth noting that no evidence has come down to us from luthiers of the past that wood was stored for extraordinary lengths of time or that wood a hundred years old is acoustically superior to wood five years old.

Backs are made of maple cut on the quarter or slab, and price is governed by age and degree of flame or curl. Imported wood is expensive and can be had from dealers in violin wood.

Tops and backs are normally sold as a partly sawed-through wedge to guarantee book matching of the halves. They are sawed apart and their bottom face smoothed level. Edges are jointed by clamping a half flat on top of a wide board, the center joint jutting out slightly from the edge. A long jointing or jack plane laid on its side is run along the edge to plane it smooth. Jointing can also be done by rubber-cementing butted strips of #100 grit garnet paper to the edge of a perfectly straight board or metal level. The sanding edge is rubbed against the jointing edge until smooth. When both halves can be butted without light being visible through the joint, they are ready to be glued.

Plane the outside long edges of the top dead straight but angle one edge so that the top becomes a slightly tapered rectangle. Saw out a ³/₄" piece of plywood 3" larger all around than your top. Glue a 1" x 3" board along one long edge and position the top against this edge. Glue another 1" x 3" board on the other side exactly coincident with the other long edge of the top. You now have a wedge-shaped gluing jig with the same taper as the top. Apply a thin coat of clear epoxy to the jointed edges of the top and position it in the jig over a slip sheet of wax paper. Tap the top into the wedge with a hammer until the center joint is wedged tightly together. Apply clamps over the joint to make sure it remains

131. *Roughing out back with large gouge*

132. *Violin back with round bottom violin maker's planes*

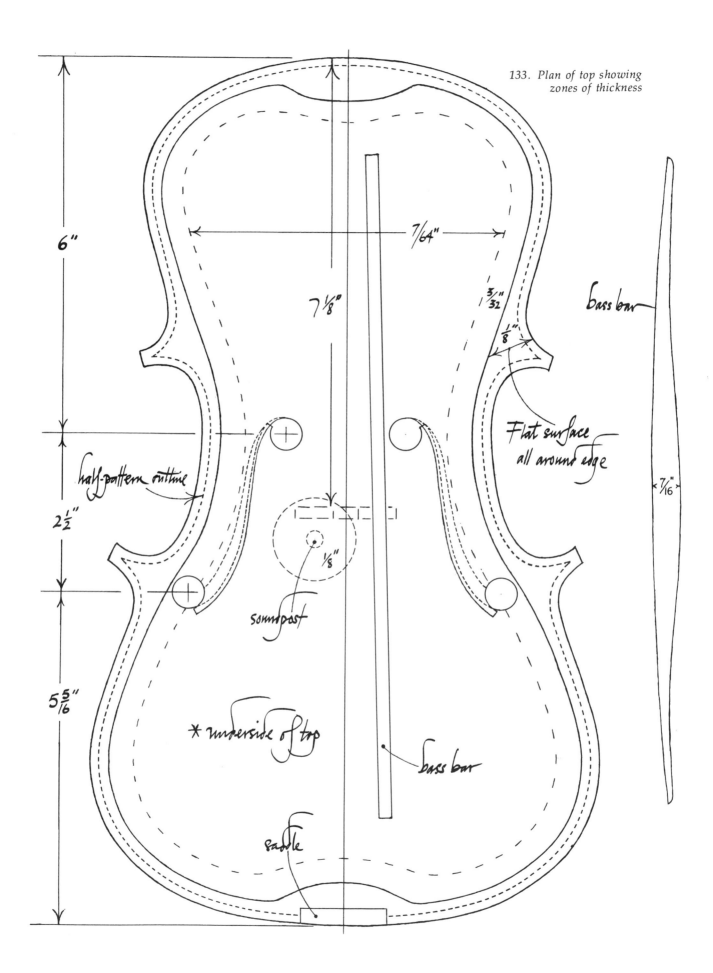

133. *Plan of top showing
zones of thickness*

6"

7/64"

7 1/8"

3/32"

1/8"

bass bar

half-pattern outline

Flat surface
all around edge

2 1/2"

7/16"

1/8"

soundpost

5 5/16"

* underside of top

bass bar

saddle

flat and leave overnight.

The back is jointed and glued in the same manner.

Remove the top from the jig and position your half pattern on the level face. Find or make a metal washer of approximately 5/16" diameter with a small center hole into which a ballpoint pen can be inserted. Size the washer so that when the pen is in place and you run it around the half pattern, it makes a line at least 5/32" away from the pattern. This line marks the edge of the top and includes an allowance of slightly over 3/32" for overhang. Hardanger fiddles seem generally to use a smaller overhang than the standard violin, sometimes as little as 1/16".

Trace the full contour of the top with the washer setup and check the outline against your completed rib frame with prop in place. If the ribs and linings were correctly bent and the mold was symmetrical, there should be no problem. Discrepancies must be resolved by altering the rib frame or the top contour or, perhaps, a bit of both.

Clamp the rib frame in place and trace the entire inner contour. Remove the frame and saw out the contour of the top with an adjustable coping saw and file the contour smooth. Lay the top flat on a smooth surface. Rest a pencil on some veneer scraps to elevate the point 3/16" above the table surface. Hold the pencil there and slowly revolve the edge of the top against the point to trace a line around the side edge of the top. This is the edge thickness to be maintained while the top is carved.

For carving, use the gluing jig as a holding device for the top by strategically wedging or clamping small blocks of wood. Rough out the basic shape of the top with a sharp one-inch gouge struck by mallet or hammer. Angle the cutting edge for a shearing action and work across the grain especially near the wings where caution is required. Take out small chips and proceed slowly until you gain more confidence with the gouge. After the rough arching is completed with gouge and the edge is down to the 3/16" line, continue with a small violin maker's plane or gooseneck scraper to refine the modeling.

Templates and arching guides are used by some makers but I prefer the freehand method for arching the plates, guided only by eye and my sense of how it should look. There is nothing immutable about violin shape or arching, within reasonable physical limits, that should inhibit your esthetic judgment. We know, for example, that Stradivari often altered his violins' shape, size, plate thicknesses, arching, and rib height. Arching templates were then unknown, each maker being guided by his artistic instincts.

Violin plates are traditionally tap-tuned by their makers to establish their resonant pitch. If you hold a plate at the top edge and tap it with your knuckles just below the bridge area you can—if your hearing is very good—determine its approximate pitch. The purpose is to bring the pitch of top and back into some acoustic accord that will produce a violin with a good tone.

Wide disagreement exists as to which tones the plates should be pitched to and no substantive testing has been done on violins made by first-rank old makers. In 1840, Felix Savart, a French investigator into the theory of vibrating strings and surfaces, reported that tuning both plates to the same pitch produced a bad violin.

My own belief is that tapping a plate was employed by the old masters as a general way of gauging acoustic quality and not for the purpose of establishing any formal harmonic pairing of the plates. They were on intensely intimate terms with the nature and tonal properties of the woods they used and probably built each violin with a preconceived notion of how thick the plates should be, given the wood being used. For a luthier who has built many violins, a more reliable indicator than ambiguous tap tones might be pressing in the plates with a thumb to test their degree of elasticity. A school of violin building has sprung up which uses audio frequency generators and oscilloscopes working within certain parameters and median figures to "tune" plates more accurately. Their claim is that this technique will help prevent building a bad violin. Perhaps it works, but even if it does, an ineluctable corollary is that it almost certainly will help prevent building a great violin. Making great things

134. Drilling holes for different depth zones in back

135. Rough carving interior of belly

136. *Flexible scraper blade with curved edge
used to true curved surfaces*

137. *Clock caliper gives accurate millimeter
reading of plate thickness*

involves risks and failures that parameters and median figures neatly circumscribe.

Finish the arching of the top with scraper blade and garnet paper. Draw in the zonal areas denoting the different thicknesses, on the back of the top.

Fasten a $1/4''$ machine bolt to the center hole of a drill press table using large washers and a nut above and below the table to hold the bolt rigidly on center. File and polish the upright end of the bolt to a shiny round tip. Adjust the locknuts or depth stop to arrest the downward travel of the spindle so that it always drills the same depth hole. For the $7/64''$ zone of the belly, set the drill to stop at $9/64''$, just $1/32''$ short. This thin margin is left for finishing by hand to the right depth. Test drill a block of wood to be sure the hole depth is accurately set. Drill closely spaced holes all over the $7/64''$ zone keeping a bit away from the zone outline. Reset the drill depth to $1/8''$ to drill the $3/32''$ zone holes.

Rest the top on some rubber padding or an old blanket, and clamp one end over a padded support (135). Carve out the belly with gouge, small plane, and gooseneck scraper. When all the holes are barely visible, you are down to the $1/32''$ margin. Remove this last layer carefully, checking frequently with calipers. Clock calipers make this simple, and as the right depth is achieved in an area, mark it with an X. Sand both sides of the top with fine garnet paper.

Lay the half pattern on the flat side of the back and use the washer and ballpoint pen to trace the full contour of the back. At the top center, add the button to which the heel of the neck will glue. Clamp the rib frame in place and trace down the entire inner contour. Cut out the back and pencil the $3/16''$ line around the perimeter as before. Carve the back to shape using the same techniques employed for the top.

138. Partly finished top with goose neck scraper

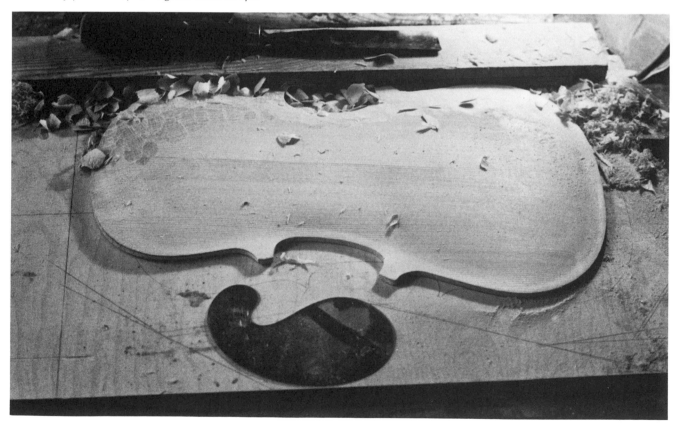

118

139. *Plan of back showing thickness zones*

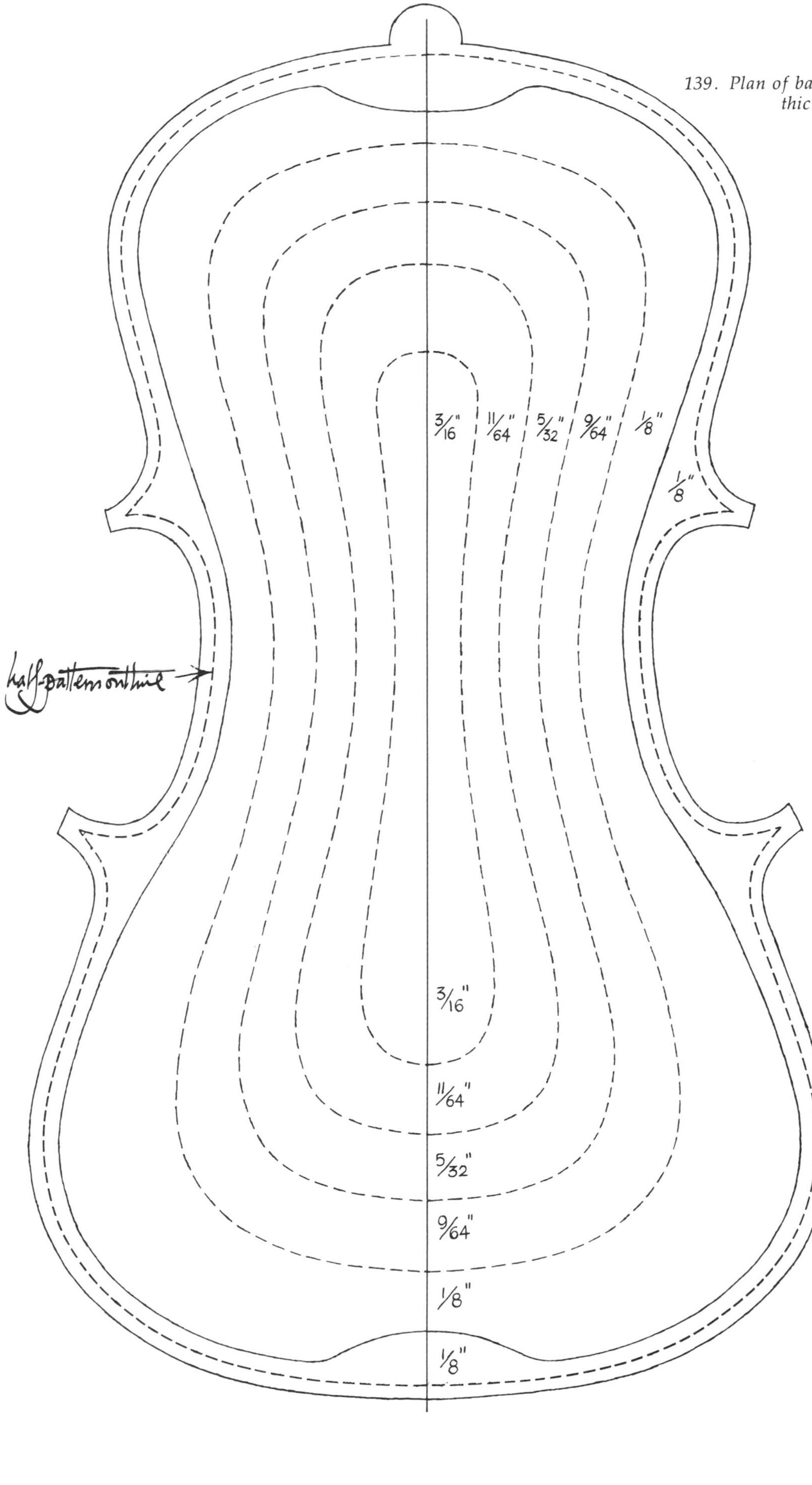

3/16" | 11/64" | 5/32" | 9/64" | 1/8"

1/8"

half-pattern outline →

3/16"

11/64"

5/32"

9/64"

1/8"

1/8"

119

F-holes

Hardanger fiddles have an overlapping f-hole of mysterious origin. Were they just a tricky effect that appealed to a provincial eye? Or did the early makers imagine that they offered some acoustic benefit? No one knows for sure, but my own surmise is that the first theory is closer to the mark. These difficult f-holes were, undoubtedly, a hallmark that makers took pride in, and their careful execution was a measure of the maker's skill.

The manner in which these f-holes were made is also a mystery. I am convinced that they were not carved into the top, a method that would have made the carving of the top an extraordinarily difficult job. After close study of several old fiddles, I have

140. Completed fiddle showing overlapped f-hole

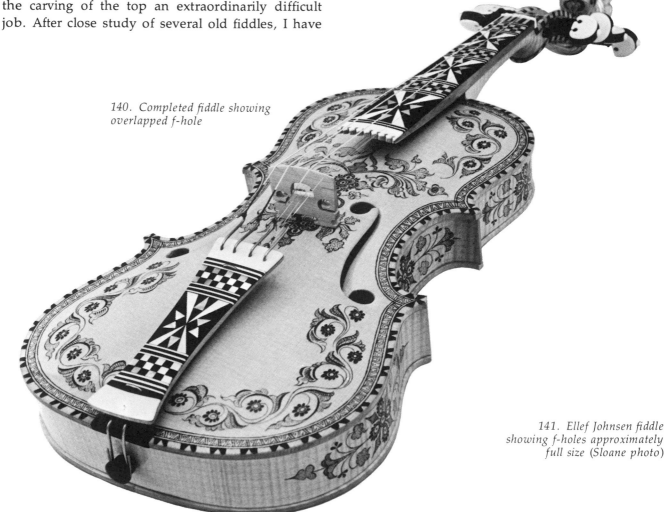

141. Ellef Johnsen fiddle showing f-holes approximately full size (Sloane photo)

120

come to the conclusion that the f-hole was an oblique cut made between the end holes that was then artificially spread to achieve the overlapping effect. Moreover, the unusually large end holes support the theory of artificial separation because they tend to minimize the chance of splitting the top if the f-hole is wedged apart. On some fiddles the spread is as much as 3/8".

Proceeding on this theory, I drew the f-holes in place and cut out the end holes with a razor-sharp knife similar to a scalpel. I was afraid to use a large-diameter drill on the delicate soundboard. Then I cut the long connecting slot at a 45 degree angle to the top. Working slowly and after innumerable slices with the knife, I broke through to the back. All the feather edges were trimmed to a blunt edge with the knife. At this stage only rudimentary cleaning up of the f-holes was done, the final shaping postponed until after the spreading of the slots.

The f-hole areas were moistened by placing a wet sponge on both sides of each f-hole and weighting it with a board to make sure the sponges were squeezed into good contact. After about an hour of damping, I removed the sponges and inserted small felt wedges into the slots to gradually force them apart. The wedges were about two inches long with a gradual taper that permitted pulling them through from the underside of the top. When the opening in the slots was large enough, I inserted a 3/16" x 3/4" x 4 1/2" wooden slat through one slot and out the other. The slat was carefully rounded on both edges so that in cross-section it appears somewhat elliptical. To prevent any general distortion of the top that might result from this stress, I clamped the top to the mold in eight places. It was left to dry for three days.

The size of the gap possible in an f-hole depends on the carving of the top. If the top is carved to drop off rather steeply at the f-hole location with an exaggerated valley or scoop at the bottom, a large gap is easily possible. The only advantage I see in a large gap is that it makes placement of the soundpost much easier.

If you are not happy with your gap, the wetting and wedging operation can be repeated using thicker wedging and a thicker slat. The moisture will not affect the epoxy-glued center joint, and the only thing you have to worry about is cracking the top through abrupt or excessive pressure.

After the top was dry, the f-holes were carefully trimmed with a sharp knife to their final appearance. The free ends were squared off and leading edges thinned to about 1/16". The long bevel was smoothed with a fine flat file. It is standard practice to cut violin f-holes using only a knife because it offers the best chance for precision. If you use a file or sandpaper to true the edges of an f-hole you will quickly learn why this is true. The softer, white springwood in the annular divisions of the wood will wear away faster than the harder, darker summerwood when subjected to abrasive action, leaving a ragged edge.

Bass Bar

Bass bars on early violins were carved in relief out of the back of the soundboard. Gradually, they evolved into a separate piece that has been enlarged over the years to make it stronger. A higher playing pitch, heightened bridge, and longer string length all contributed to an increase in the pressure on the top, necessitating a stronger bass bar to prevent collapse of the belly. The basic function of the bass bar is to transmit to the soundboard the vibrations of the left foot of the bridge and compensate for dif-

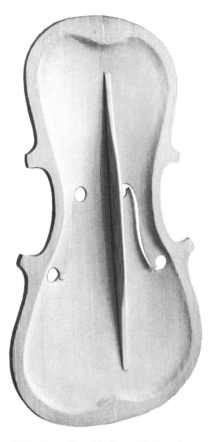

ferences in the resonant pitch of the soundboard caused by cutting the sound holes.

Cut a piece of straight-grained spruce to $3/16''$ thick x $9/16''$ high x $10^{1}/2''$ long. The grain should run parallel to the $9/16''$ dimension, the same as the grain of the top. Mark lightly the exact position of the bass bar on the back of the top. Looking at the back of the top, its position will be on your right. Place the bar in position and pencil a rough approximation of the curved surface underneath it on the side of the bar. Trim the ends so that the center of the bar is less than $1/16''$ from the belly. Hold the bar in place with one hand and slide a one-inch stub of pencil along the belly so that the pencil point traces the curve onto the side of the bass bar. Plane the bottom edge to this contour and fit the bar to the exact curve of the belly. Shave it with a scraper blade until it makes contact with the belly at every point. Glue in place with Titebond and deep throat clamps. Trim the bass bar to the final shape shown in the blueprint.

142. *Completed belly with bass bar*

143. *Gluing in bass bar*

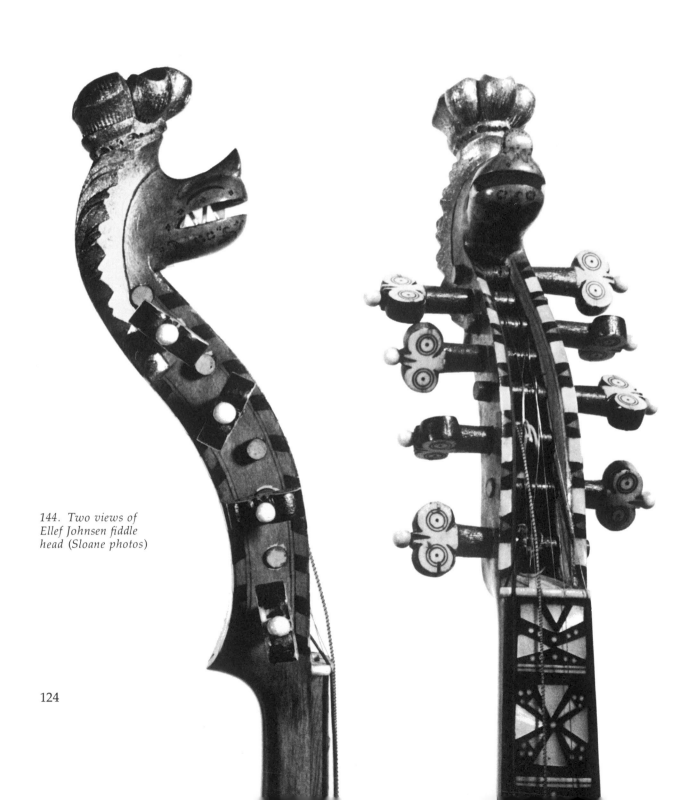

144. Two views of
Ellef Johnsen fiddle
head (Sloane photos)

124

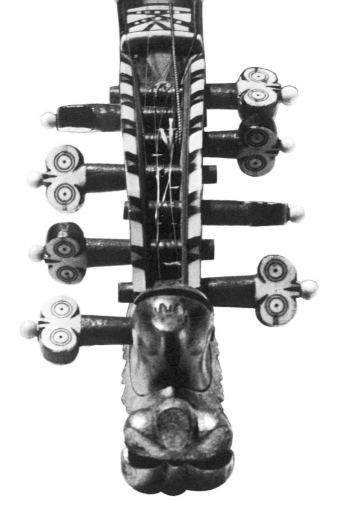

145. Another view showing crown detail and nut notched for passage of sympathetic strings

Neck and Peg Box

Cut the neck from a block of maple 1½" x 2½" x 12". Draw the shape of the dragon head, peg box, and neck on the side of the block. The dragon head, a recurrent motif in Scandinavian folk art, is often carved with bone teeth (set in later) and protruding tongue, features I have omitted from my design.

Saw out the back and front contours of the block with a bandsaw or coping saw. Save the back piece, which will serve as a support when carving the head and peg box. Drill eight ¼" holes for the pegs and draw the peg box and neck shape on the front of the block. Saw off the long tapered piece on each side of the neck and peg box, leaving a small margin of extra wood on the neck portion.

Saw off as much surplus wood from the head as you can with a coping saw before starting with a chisel. Rest the neck in the saved back support cushioned by a thin sheet of rubber or leather to compensate for the wood that became sawdust. This ensemble can be clamped upright in a vise or horizontally, in which case rubber bands can be used to secure the neck to the support. Carve the crown first. Use chisel and file to define the shapes, periodically sighting down the neck from the head to maintain symmetry. Carve the scooped-out part behind the jaw to bring into relief the stylized mane. The entire mane is carved as a round, blank entity and the head carving completed before the veining is done. Beware of getting the head too small. It will weaken the final appearance of the fiddle if the head looks disproportionately small. The head is a powerful device and should be executed boldly.

To carve out the peg box cavity use the drilling system used to simplify the carving of the plates. Set the drill to leave a ⁵/₃₂" thickness of wood in the peg box back and drill a lot of ³/₁₆" holes in the peg box. During drilling, hold the neck so that the plane of the peg box resting on the bolt is always at right

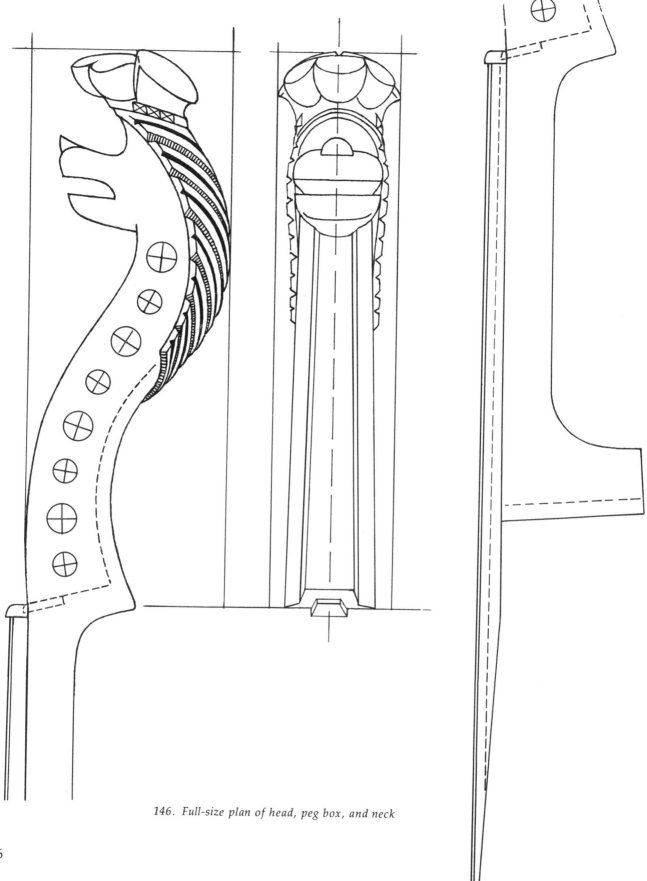

146. *Full-size plan of head, peg box, and neck*

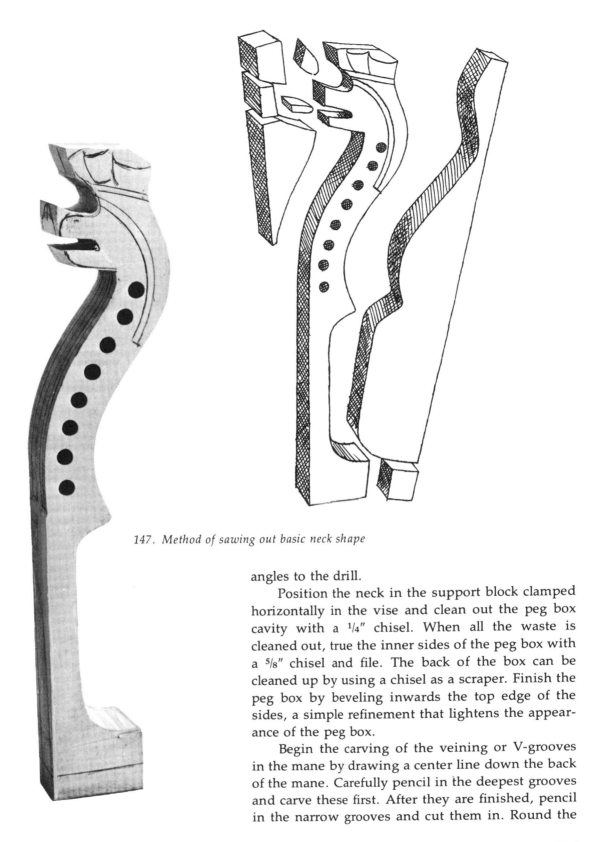

147. *Method of sawing out basic neck shape*

angles to the drill.

Position the neck in the support block clamped horizontally in the vise and clean out the peg box cavity with a ¼" chisel. When all the waste is cleaned out, true the inner sides of the peg box with a ⁵⁄₈" chisel and file. The back of the box can be cleaned up by using a chisel as a scraper. Finish the peg box by beveling inwards the top edge of the sides, a simple refinement that lightens the appearance of the peg box.

Begin the carving of the veining or V-grooves in the mane by drawing a center line down the back of the mane. Carefully pencil in the deepest grooves and carve these first. After they are finished, pencil in the narrow grooves and cut them in. Round the underside of the neck and carve the heel to shape but do not cut off the surplus wood at the bottom of the neck. This portion is not cut off until the neck is fitted to the body. Smooth the entire neck and head with fine garnet paper and riffler files to get into narrow recesses in the dragon carving.

Cut the small mortise at the bottom of the peg box which will carry the ivory nut for the sympathetic strings. Cut and fit the nut but do not glue it in.

Norwegian fiddle makers used gold or bronze paint for gilding the crown and mane, but I prefer to use gold leaf. Bronzing paints are sold in art supply stores but will not give a result anywhere nearly as attractive as leaf.

148. Fiddle head, anonymous (Smithsonian Collection, Sloane photo)

A wood carving, no matter how carefully smoothed, cannot be leaf-gilded successfully unless the wood is covered with gesso to transform it into a hard, absorbent surface that will permit burnishing. Gesso gilding was a highly refined art during the Middle Ages and recipes for gilding and the illuminating of manuscripts have come down to us most notably through Cennino Cennini's *The Craftsman's Handbook,* a fifteenth-century treatise on artists' materials and techniques.

After the figurehead was chiseled and smoothed to a careful finish it was clamped upright in the vise without the back support. Rabbit glue in granular form (or calfskin glue) was dissolved in a double boiler—1 teaspoon of glue to 3 tablespoons of water. I use a small Pyrex glass bowl seated in the top of a small saucepan as a double boiler. The mixture must be stirred while the water heats. As the solution heats up, the glue will dissolve, but the glue solution must not be allowed to boil. Stir continuously until the glue is thoroughly dissolved.

Apply the glue while still warm to the crown and mane with a small artist's brush. After several hours apply a second coat and allow a day's drying time. Prepare another batch of glue and add a tablespoon or slightly more of whiting (powdered calcium carbonate). Mix these together off the heat but while the glue is still warm. Mix to a smooth consistency with a liquidity approaching heavy cream. This is now gesso, a white filler held together with a

128

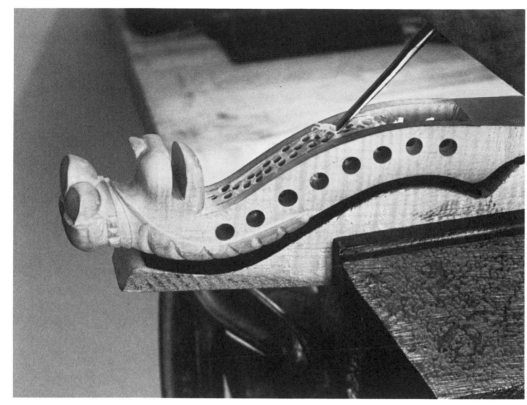

149. Chiseling out peg box waste after drilling

glue binder. Paint a coat of gesso on the glue-coated areas with a small brush. In a few hours this gesso coating will solidify to a hard white substance with a matte appearance. It can be carved and sanded with much more precision and refinement than wood. I gave my figurehead three coats of gesso with some carving and slight sanding between coats to avoid the loss of small detail.

The final coat was allowed to dry a full day and final carving and smoothing was completed using small chisels, riffler files, and sandpaper. When all surfaces were perfectly smooth, I used an agate burnisher to burnish all exposed surfaces to a high glossy sheen. Gesso has a slight tooth and springiness that permits burnishing to a marble finish, an ideal surface for laying down gold leaf.

Mordants, the adhesives used to adhere gold leaf to gesso, are sold in art supply stores as bronzing liquids. They are essentially varnishes with good leveling properties and a predictable tack stage at which point the leaf is applied. The liquid is applied with a small artist's brush and allowed to dry

to the tack stage. Gold leaf is applied as described in drum decoration (page 168).

Gold leaf applied directly onto gesso with a commercially prepared bronzing liquid cannot be successfully burnished to a high metallic luster. In order to do this the gesso must first be coated with a gilder's clay or bole which has some glue mixed into it. Several coats are used and smoothed carefully to a fine finish. Leaf is applied to the clay-coated surface by first brushing on some water, which activates the glue, producing sufficient tack to adhere the leaf. This kind of gilding can be burnished to a high luster with an agate burnisher. The soft luster produced by the leaf-on-gesso method is more appropriate to a violin figurehead than a really high metallic shine, and much superior to bronze paint.

I gave my figurehead two coats of gold leaf. The neck is complete, at this point, except for the reaming of the peg holes and the final finishing that follows installation of the fingerboard. It must be handled with care and guarded against knocks that might fracture the gesso.

150. *View of assembled fiddle*

*151. Full-size inlay pattern
for fingerboard*

Fingerboard and Tailpiece

Hardanger fiddle fingerboards are almost flat and I curved mine to a radius of $9^{1}/_{4}''$. The fingerboard is a composite of a thin layer of marquetry glued to a wedge-shaped board. On early fiddles, the neck was fastened in line with the horizontal plane of the body. Angling of the fingerboard to elevate the strings to bridge height was accomplished with this wedge. The wedge makes fingering difficult in the higher registers because the neck gets much thicker near the body. This is not a problem for Hardanger fiddle players; their music confines them pretty much to the first position. But by 1800, the demands of modern violin technique forced the discarding of the wedge in favor of a neck of uniform thickness set in at an angle. Hardanger fiddles after the 1860's exhibit a modified wedge combined with an angled neck, and this is the compromise I adopted.

The marquetry facing is made up of ebony, ivory, and mother-of-pearl. Norwegian fiddle makers used horn and bone in place of ebony and ivory. For the ebony, I sawed a $^{1}/_{4}''$ x $1^{1}/_{2}''$ x $7''$ block of ebony in half through the $^{1}/_{4}''$ dimension. This gave me two pieces I filed and scraped to a thickness of $^{1}/_{16}''$. The pearl was purchased in

131

152. *Partially completed montage of inlay pieces glued to backing of heavy vellum (vegetable parchment)*

roughly 1″ x 2″ blanks of .060″ thickness, and the ivory came from piano key facings.

Draw your fingerboard design, keeping in mind the following: (a) the inlay pieces must be arranged to preserve the vertical articulation of the facing so that it will bend to the curve of the fingerboard without breaking; (b) avoid a design that brings the point of, say, a star to the edge of the fingerboard—it will break off; (c) if you use a horizontal design element that runs from edge to edge, it will have to be kerfed—partly sawn through at intervals—on the back.

On my fingerboard, I made use of a five-ply ivory-ebony sandwich that horizontally separated major design elements. These were all kerfed in about eight places on the gluing side. Single horizontal elements will bend without kerfing, and pearl cannot be used as a horizontal edge-to-edge element—it will break.

Make a careful drawing of your design on a sheet of tracing paper and then trace this design onto a sheet of heavy vellum tracing paper. This parchment-type tracing paper is sold in art supply shops and is the backing to which the marquetry facing will be glued.

Use the lightweight tracing paper to transfer the design to the ebony, ivory, and pearl. Carbon paper works well for ivory and pearl, white typewriter correction paper will work for ebony. Cut out all the

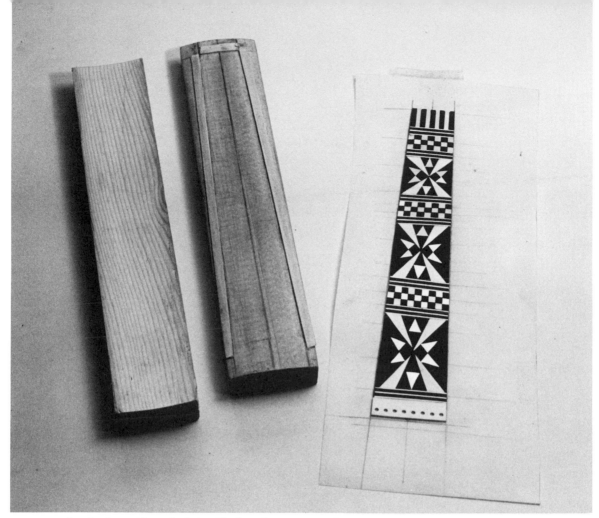

153. *Completed inlay with neck gluing block and concave caul*

pieces with a jeweler's saw. (See banjo inlay, page 46.) Paste them into place on the vellum, filling in all the spaces like a puzzle.

A checkerboard pattern of ebony and pearl is made by cutting three pieces of ebony and three pieces of pearl each 1½″ long by whatever width the squares will be. Each length must be precisely the same width. Glue up two assemblies, one with ebony outer strips and a pearl center strip, the other with pearl outer strips and an ebony center strip. Edge-glue with epoxy by positioning each assembly on a piece of wax paper over a board, and using push pins to squeeze them together. When dry, cut them into segments and alternate them to get a checkerboard effect. In my design I used squares of slightly different size for the different units to avoid halving a segment.

Absolute precision is not necessary—or pos-sible—in cutting and fitting the marquetry elements because the lampblack and epoxy filler applied afterwards will conceal all defects. It is helpful to have the pearl, ivory, and ebony of reasonably proximate thickness before cutting. Glue all the pieces to the vellum with white glue applied sparingly to prevent glue from seeping up through the crevices and edge-gluing pieces.

When the entire assembly is completed, trim off the vellum close to the facing. This completed face is the side that will be glued to the spruce wedge that is, in fact, the fingerboard. Carefully file it level over its entire face. Individual sections can be filed separately by flexing the inlay. Horizontal elements can be kerfed by simply folding back the inlay on each side of the element. Avoid filing the facing too thin because some filing will be required on the reverse side after the facing is glued down.

133

If you are using my marquetry design, drill the 1/16" holes at the bottom zig-zag cutout but do not cut out the points. These are cut out after the facing is glued and the fingerboard completed.

Prepare a fingerboard of straight-grained quartersawn spruce 1/2" x 2" x 9½". Round the surface to a 9¼" radius using as a guide a template cut out to this radius. Draw the shape of the fingerboard on this rounded face, centered on the block. Glue a thin strip of veneer along the top and side edges as a retainer strip to keep the facing from shifting when it is glued down. Prepare a wooden caul the same size as the fingerboard with a concave radius that matches the curve of the fingerboard.

Mix some epoxy with enough powdered lamp-black to color it black. Smear this mixture over the face of the marquetry strip and position it on the fingerboard vellum side up. Cover it with a sheet of freezer wrap or wax paper. Over this lay a thin sheet of rubber at least as wide as the facing, and then the fitted caul. The rubber sheet is designed to equalize the pressure if all your inlay parts are not the same thickness. Apply a clamp to each end of the ensemble and lock the center portion in a vise to get good clamping pressure throughout.

Leave overnight to dry. The next day, remove the fingerboard and strip off the vellum backing. Remove the veneer strips around the edge. Use a fine flat single-cut file to smooth the facing level. If you use fine garnet paper, fasten it to a long block of wood. Mix some more filler and fill all crevices. Allow to dry and repeat the filling operation until all crevices arc gone and the facing presents a smooth, unbroken expanse from top to bottom. If you are using the zig-zag cutout in your design, avoid filling the drill holes.

Saw out the shape of the fingerboard, smoothing the sides and top flush with the facing edge. For the zig-zag cutout, cut the wood off flush with the ends of the points. Draw the wedge profile on the side of the fingerboard and saw it out. Save the sawed-off piece to make the tailpiece. Chisel out the cavity underneath the fingerboard to make room for the sympathetic strings. Use a small gouge, gooseneck scraper, and sandpaper to make this cavity.

The tailpiece is made from the portion cut from the bottom of the fingerboard or a 1/4" x 2" x 5½" spruce block. It is arched to the same radius as the fingerboard and the marquetry facing is handled in the same way. Eight 1/16" holes must be drilled for the steel wire crooks that hold the strings and secure the tailpiece to the tail button.

154. *Full-size pattern for tailpiece*

155. *Close-up of nut section*

156. *Underside view of wired tailpiece and completed fingerboard*

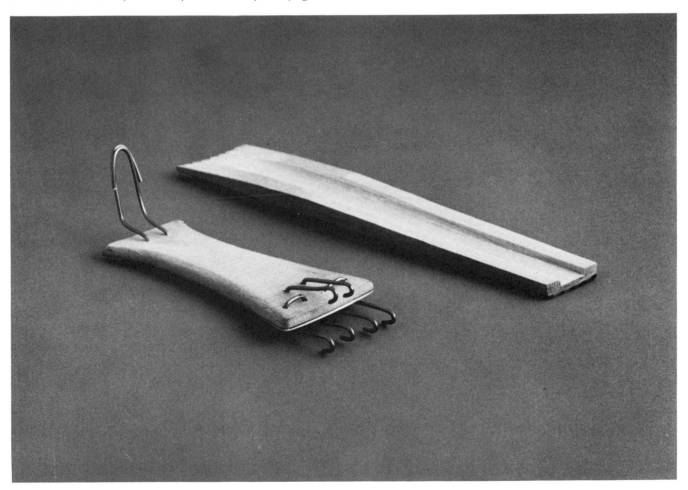

*157. Gluing top to rib frame
with small clamps over
leather cauls*

Assembling Body

Position the top on the rib frame, making sure it is correctly aligned with a uniform edge overhang all around. Clamp the top in this position and mark for drilling points at opposite ends of the top, each spot just clear of the center joint and $3/8''$ from the edge. Drill each hole with a $1/16''$ drill going about $1/2''$ into the end blocks. Two round toothpicks are used to pin the top accurately and quickly in place when gluing it on the rib frame. Remove the top, reverse the rib frame and drill the holes for pinning the back in the same manner as the top.

Animal or hide glue is used for gluing the plates to the rib frame because its water solubility makes it easy to remove the plates for repair if nec-

essary. Hide glue is sold in granular form for mixing by the user. (See gilding, page 128.) It is also available in prepared liquid form sold in hardware stores (Franklin Hide Glue). I mixed my own glue but see nothing wrong in using a liquid hide glue. This glue has a slower setting time than hot glue, an important advantage that will give you more time for assembly.

Glue the back on first. Thin the glue to an easy-flowing consistency and apply it to the top edges of the ribs and linings, and the blocks. Apply it also to the gluing edge of the back, using a small brush. Let it dry thoroughly and give the blocks a second coat if they look like they need it. Have at least ten small clamps handy along with a pair of leather cauls for each clamp, and some round toothpicks.

Brush the glue over all the gluing edges, pin the

136

back in place with the toothpicks, and apply the clamps. If you are using a hot glue, work in a warm room to gain some assembly time before the glue gels. Apply the clamps with just enough pressure to bring the joint into tight contact without distorting the ribs. If you find an unglued portion when the glue has dried, place a drop of water in the joint. Squeeze the top against the rib to force the water along the joint and work some fresh glue into the crack with a thin spatula and clamp. Clean away glue ooze with a clean, damp cloth. Make sure the inside of the box is smooth and clean before signing your name on the back. Glue the top to the rib frame in the same manner.

When both plates are properly glued on, finish the toothpicks flush with the plates. Check the overhang for uniformity and file away uneven spots. On many Hardanger fiddles the bottom edge of the overhang is rounded off, on others the top and bottom edges are both rounded slightly.

Cut the mortise for the saddle and make an ebony saddle. Fit it to a tight fit by cutting the saddle slightly oversize, reducing it gradually to size. Glue in place with Titebond.

158. Clamping arrangement for gluing fingerboard to neck

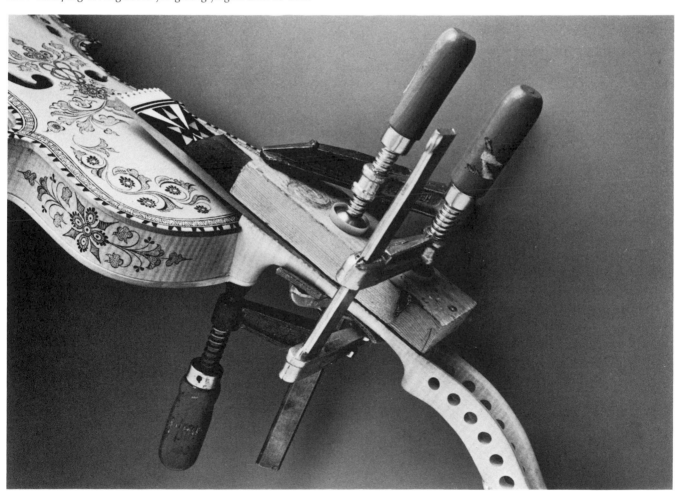

Joining Neck to Body

Saw off the surplus wood at the bottom end of the neck and the bottom of the heel, leaving a slight margin of extra wood. Shape the heel to its final contour, taking care that both sides are symmetrical. Mark the center line of the neck block and cut off that portion of the top overhang where the neck will be mortised. From each edge of this opening draw a line across the ribs to the bottom edge. These two guidelines must be parallel to the center line.

Butt the neck against the body, centered between the lines, and trace down its contour. Draw the shape of the mortise on the top and drill two $3/16''$ holes to facilitate chiseling out the mortise. Cut the mortise to a tight fit that requires gradual enlargement to seat the neck. In this way you can seat the neck so snugly that it will remain in position unsupported. The bottom of the heel must fit squarely against the button. If your neck angle is correct, the lower end of the fingerboard will have its top face $11/16''$ from the surface of the soundboard. Affix the fingerboard to the neck with a small clamp to check this.

If the end of the fingerboard is not $11/16''$ above the surface, you should be able to achieve this distance by increasing the angle of wedge under the fingerboard. The only thing to guard against here is narrowing too much the depth of the tunnel through which the sympathetic strings must pass. It may be better to increase the angle of the neck if the tunnel looks like it is already narrow enough.

Once the proper relationship is established between the neck, fingerboard, and body, they are separated. Gluing of the neck and fingerboard are postponed until after all inlay and drawing are completed. It is infinitely more convenient to draw on the neck and the body while they are separate.

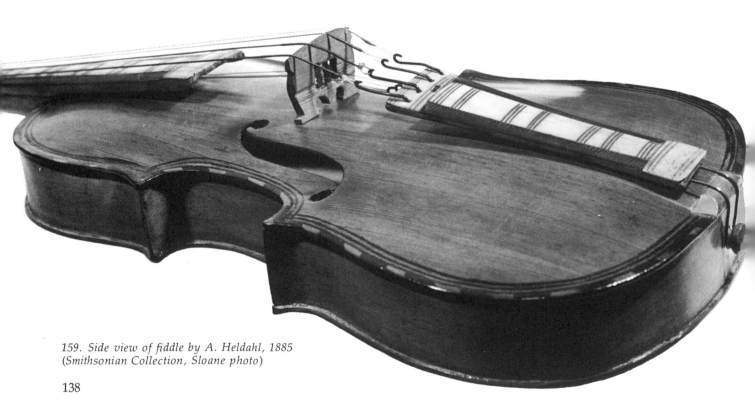

159. Side view of fiddle by A. Heldahl, 1885
(Smithsonian Collection, Sloane photo)

160. Front view of completed fiddle

Decoration

Except for a few minor details, my surface drawings are copied from the Ellef Johnsen fiddle (115). His drawings have an airy Spencerian grace reminiscent of Pennsylvania Dutch *fraktur* work. This graceful style is a hallmark of the Helland family and many of the design elements recur in slightly different form in their fiddles. I omitted Johnsen's use of pearl inlay around the edge of the top and peg box, thinking it could be added at some future date. It is much easier to do beforehand, however, so if you are using pearl inlay do it before any surface drawing is done. (See banjo inlay, page 46.)

The drawings I have examined on old fiddles, including the Johnsen fiddle, appear to have been done extemporaneously. Major elements, such as a flower, were probably drawn in first as a skeletal framework for drawing in the rest of the design. For a novice, it is prudent to make a careful rendering of the design and trace it in position on the fiddle.

Sand the entire body smooth with fine garnet paper and then go over it with a clean, damp cloth. This will raise the grain and in about an hour you can sand it to a super-smooth finish. The body must then be given a wash coat of shellac (1 part shellac, 5 parts alcohol) to seal the surface and keep India ink from fuzzing into the grain. Shellac has a short shelf life and after repeated disappointments with prepared shellacs that never dry, I now make my own. Shellac is sold in granular form or buttons and is dissolved in denatured alcohol to make the familiar cloudy solution. The cloudiness is caused by imperfectly soluble waxes contained in shellac which dry transparent in a shellac coating. A white refined dewaxed grade of shellac is sold by Behlen & Bros. (See Suppliers, page 159.)

I tinted the wash coat by adding a pinch of an alcohol-soluble aniline dye color, Bismarck brown. Application was by mouth-blown spray pipe, which gives a perfectly uniform coat that can be repeated in fifteen minutes to get a deeper tone. This cannot be done with a brush without streaking the finish.

Make your tracing into a transfer paper by coat-

139

ing the back with a soft 5B graphite pencil. Rub the pencil back and forth until there is a jet black layer of graphite on the paper. Wet a small wad of absorbent cotton with some benzol or naphtha and squeeze it almost dry. Pad the graphite-covered area very briskly until there is a uniform coverage of dark gray and all the excess graphite is on the pad. This rubbing process makes a smudge-proof transfer sheet. Test it on a piece of paper to see if you get a good line image. If not, the blacking and padding operation can be repeated. This kind of graphite transfer paper can be erased easily—typewriter carbon paper cannot.

Start on the back of the fiddle first. Scotch-tape your tracing in position and trace it down lightly with nothing harder than a 2H pencil. Avoid making a debossed line in the wood surface. Draw in the design with a small artist's brush or pen, whichever you feel most comfortable with. I used both a #1 brush and a crow quill pen. Proceed with care because mistakes or blots are hard to undo. When the drawing is finished, erase any graphite tracing lines still showing. As each section is completed— back, ribs, top—give it a coat of varnish. Use a good grade of clear violin oil varnish applied with a soft-haired brush. Be careful around the f-holes to avoid dripping varnish into the interior.

161. Back view showing head detail and surface decoration

140

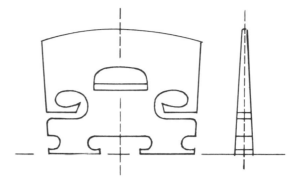

*162. Full-size plan of bridge
with small ivory inset as saddle
for sympathetic strings*

Assembly

Glue the neck into the mortise after making sure it is exactly centered on the longitudinal axis of the fiddle. This can be checked by fixing the neck in the mortise slot and aligning a thin flexible metal rule or wooden slat with the neck and belly center line. If the mortise is a loose fit, you might be able to wedge it with thin veneer strips to permit checking the neck alignment without worrying about the neck falling off. Misalignment of the neck is corrected by filing off slightly one side of the neck face that butts against the front of the mortise slot. Glue the neck in place with Titebond and a clamp applied over the top of the mortise and under the button.

If you are using the fingerboard zig-zag cutout, redrill the holes and saw out the points, leaving at least $3/32"$ of wood under the points. Fasten the fingerboard in place with some masking tape and fit the ivory nut. Position the small nut that carries the sympathetic strings. File the top to the correct height and saw four equally spaced shallow cuts for string grooves with a jeweler's saw. Glue the nut in place with Titebond and set aside the main nut and fingerboard. They are not glued in place until after varnishing of the fiddle is completed.

Make the bridge (162) from a piece of maple with the grain running parallel to the flat plane of the fiddle. Saw it out with a jeweler's saw and clean it up with small files and fine sandpaper. Glue in the small triangular ivory saddle that will carry the

sympathetic strings.

Bend thirty-five gauge stainless steel wire (just under $1/16"$ diameter) into a U-shape and flatten the top of the U. Fit two of these into the holes for the main string crooks. Fit them so that the ends of the crooks jut out $5/8"$ from the top of the tailpiece. The two crooks for the sympathetic strings (two strings work off each crook) jut out only $1/2"$ from the edge.

Attach the wire for the lower end of the tailpiece. This wire rides over the saddle or tail rest and wraps around the tail button. Assemble all the wires and then wrap the tail button and insert it in its hole. This hole is reamed with a tapered reamer so that the tapered button wedges in place.

I made the eight pegs from standard ebony violin pegs filed flat and faced with ivory on both sides of the button. Two $7/64"$ holes were drilled in the lower center, cut through with a jeweler's saw, and finished with a file. Ivory finials—footed knobs like a tiny bolt—were turned from a $1/8"$ ivory rod and epoxied into holes drilled in the top of the pegs.

Peg holes were reamed with a peg hole reamer (#2 Morse taper pin reamer) after the pegs were shaved to a perfect round on a violin peg shaver. The peg holes were reamed to permit the pegs to protrude about $3/16"$ from the exit hole. A $1/16"$ string hole was drilled in each peg. This hole should be placed close to the entering peg hole so that when the holes become enlarged the string hole will not

163. Adjustable peg shaver

drift into the exit hole. Pegs work beautifully if pegs and holes are perfectly round and of identical taper. Pegs can be lubricated with peg soap sold by dealers in violin accessories.

Setting of the soundpost, a ¼" spruce dowel, is done with a tool bearing the straightforward name of soundpost setter. It is a simple, inexpensive device you may have to bend a bit to work with your particular f-hole. If the f-hole gap is wide enough, you may be able to manage the soundpost with a pair of tweezers.

Gauge the approximate height the soundpost should be and cut it slightly oversize. Impale it on the sharp end of the setting tool and try it in place. Adjust its length until it is gently wedged in position without spreading the plates; the pressure of the bridge will hold it in place. Sight through the tail button hole to check that the post is in vertical position. The scalloped end of the soundpost setter is used as a prod to move the ends of the soundpost. The position of the soundpost has a profound influence on the tone of the fiddle, and finding the right position may take some experimenting.

After varnishing and polishing are completed, glue on the fingerboard using hide glue (158). Glue the nut in place with a few dabs of Titebond, just enough to keep it from falling off. Fasten the tailpiece and string up the fiddle, starting with the sympathetic strings. These four understrings are of identical gauge and match a super-light electric guitar E or first string (.008"). Hardanger fiddle overstrings are unusual in that they use a half-overspun D string.

There are many tunings for the Hardanger fiddle but the most common one is standard violin tuning for the overstrings with the G string raised to A. For this tuning, the understrings are tuned D, E, F♯, A. In standard violin tuning (G, D, A, E) the F♯ on the understrings is raised to G.

A bilingual booklet, "The Hardanger Fiddle," by Sigbjørn B. Osa, can be purchased from the publisher: Musikk-Huset A/S, Karl Johansgt. 45, Oslo, Norway. This booklet contains tuning and playing instructions along with examples of popular Norwegian folk music. Hardanger fiddle strings are also available from Musikk-Huset A/S.

Violin Materials List

Top, two-piece spruce @ $4\frac{1}{2}''$ x $\frac{5}{8}''$ x 15"
Back, two-piece maple @ $4\frac{1}{2}''$ x $\frac{5}{8}''$ x 15"
Ribs, maple, three pieces @ $1\frac{3}{8}''$ x $\frac{1}{16}''$ x 15"
Linings, spruce or willow,
     four pieces @ $\frac{5}{16}''$ x $\frac{3}{32}''$ x $9\frac{1}{2}''$
         ''   ''   ''   '' $5\frac{1}{2}''$
         ''   ''   ''   '' $7\frac{1}{2}''$
4 corner blocks, spruce @ $1\frac{1}{2}''$ x 1" x $1\frac{3}{8}''$ high
Neck, maple, $1\frac{1}{2}''$ x $2\frac{1}{2}''$ x 12"

2 end blocks, spruce @ 2" x 1" x $1\frac{3}{8}''$ high
Bass bar, spruce, $\frac{3}{16}''$ x $\frac{9}{16}''$ x $10\frac{1}{2}''$
8 tuning pegs, ebony or rosewood
Spruce fingerboard block, 2" x $\frac{1}{2}''$ x $9\frac{1}{2}''$
Bridge, maple, $1\frac{1}{2}''$ x $\frac{1}{4}''$ x 2"
Ebony endpin
Ebony or ivory saddle, $\frac{1}{4}''$ x $\frac{1}{4}''$ x $1\frac{3}{8}''$
Soundpost, $\frac{1}{4}''$ spruce dowel

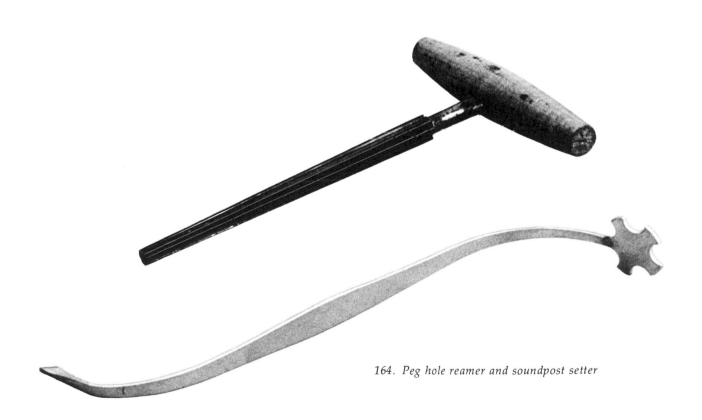

164. *Peg hole reamer and soundpost setter*

Finishing

Hardanger fiddles are sometimes made in a blond or straw-colored finish and this is the color I chose for mine. Darker colors can be achieved through the use of a deeper-toned wash coat of shellac or spirit varnish, or colored oil varnishes available in various shades of yellow, red, and brown. Varnishing and polishing of the fiddle must be done with considerable care because of the drawings.

After the initial protective coat of varnish, I applied three more coats before I began light sanding between coats with a worn piece of fine garnet paper. The gilded portion of the figurehead received only three coats in all and was not sanded or polished. Eight coats of varnish were applied to the rest of the fiddle, which was then allowed to dry thoroughly for a period of three weeks before polishing.

Apply varnish in long, even strokes with a minimum of brushing. Work in a warm room free of unsettling air currents that circulate dust. Violin makers often use a dowel through the tail button hole to hold the violin upright for varnishing and drying; the bottom of the dowel rests in a hole in the workbench. Allow a day or two between coats for drying.

After the final drying period of three weeks, the varnish is smoothed with #400 wet-or-dry silicon carbide paper and water. Dip a folded piece of the paper into water and carefully sand away all lumps and unevenness. Work under a good light and inspect the surface frequently as polishing proceeds. After initial smoothing has been accomplished, switch to #600 wet-or-dry paper and sand with water until all surface scratches are polished out. Be very careful when sanding edges, the easiest place to go through the finish. When all shiny areas (low spots) are gone and the surface has a uniform matte appearance, it is ready for final polishing. The sanding with water softens the finish and a few days of hardening should be allowed before polishing.

Powdered rottenstone and mineral oil (Johnson's Baby Oil) rubbed with a felt pad will produce a lustrous satin finish. Mix a small quantity of rottenstone with oil and dip it up with the pad. Rub it over the surface using a small circular motion. For a higher finish use water instead of oil or polish with Duco #7 Auto Polishing liquid.

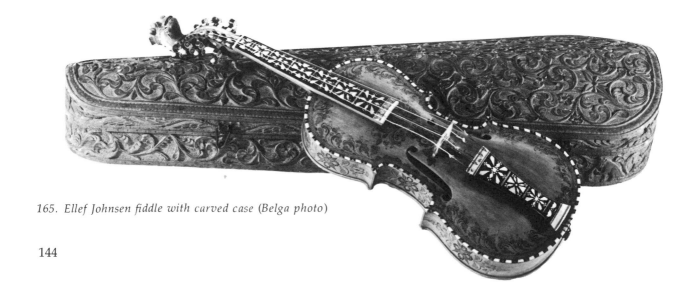

165. *Ellef Johnsen fiddle with carved case* (Belga photo)

144

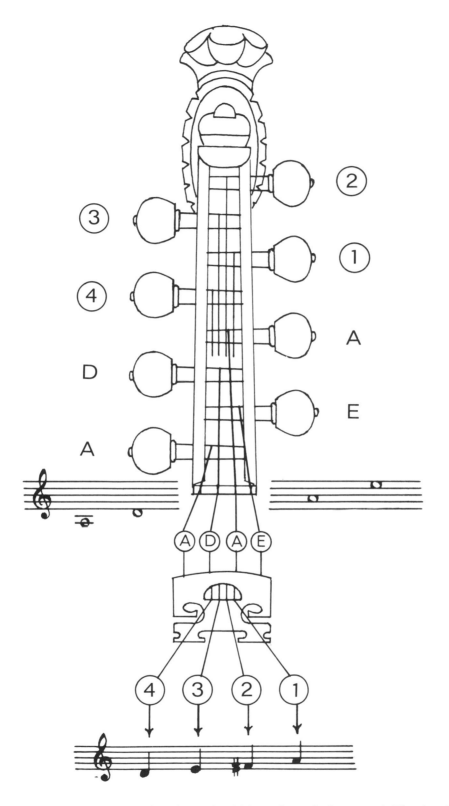

166. *Hardanger fiddles are tuned to the pitch which produces the best sound. The A string should be tuned to approximately B natural. Over twenty tunings are known, the one diagrammed above being the most common. If standard violin tuning is used (G, D, A, E) the sympathetic F sharp string is raised to G.*

The Dolmetsch Recorder

Arnold Dolmetsch (1858–1940) was born in Le Mans, France, the son of an organ builder. He received an early training in the making and repair of keyboard instruments and at age twenty-one went to Brussels to study music. From there he moved to London to enroll in the newly established Royal College of Music. His chance discovery in the college library of some early music for viols stimulated the researches that became his life's work. He began a personal crusade to bring to public notice the buried music of the sixteenth and seventeenth centuries and the ancient instruments on which this music was played.

During the 1880's he formed a family consort using viols, lute, clavichord, and harpsichord. They gave candlelight performances in period costume, musical events that attracted Bloomsbury notables including William Morris, George Moore, Aubrey Beardsley, and a music critic who became a valued supporter and friend, George Bernard Shaw. Dolmetsch built many of the instruments used in the performances.

The concerts introduced to Victorian England the works of early composers including Dowland, Locke, Vivaldi, Frescobaldi, Scarlatti, Rameau, and Couperin. Dolmetsch brought to his crusade extraordinary musical insight and a variety of useful talents. He was a gifted musician, a showman, a first-rate craftsman, but above all, an artist.

In 1917 the Dolmetsch family settled in the house at Haslemere which is still their home today. The following year, spurred by the loss of a favorite recorder by Pui Bressan, Dolmetsch decided to construct one for himself. After many experiments he succeeded in building the recorder that brought about the modern revival of interest in the recorder and its music.

The small family workshop begun in Haslemere is now Arnold Dolmetsch Ltd., a busy enterprise headed by Dr. Carl Dolmetsch. He continues in the same spirit the work his father pioneered. Early instruments made according to the principles evolved

146

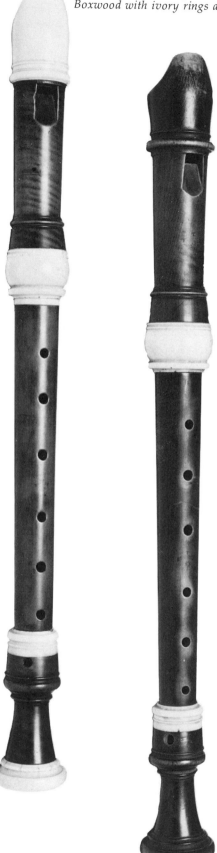

168. *Recorder in F by Pui Bressan, London, c. 1720-24.*
Boxwood with ivory rings and mouthpiece (Dolmetsch Collection).

by Arnold Dolmetsch are hand-produced in the company workshops and include harpsichords, spinets, clavichords, viols, lutes, rebecs, and tabors. The company produces a full range of superb recorders that are shipped each day to players all over the world.

Dr. Dolmetsch, the first modern recorder virtuoso, pursues an active international concert career and is also musical director of the Haslemere Festival, an annual celebration of early music begun by Arnold Dolmetsch in 1925.

Alto Recorder Construction

Numerous woods are employed for making recorders, including Honduras rosewood, boxwood, East Indian rosewood, African tulip wood, pear, grenadilla, maple, satinwood, and cherry. The wood is carefully seasoned for several years before being cut into octagonal billets to facilitate lathe turning. All the billets are drilled through and stored an additional year. For alto recorder, a ³/₄″ hole is drilled in the mouthpiece, ³/₈″ hole in the barrel, and ¹/₄″ hole in the end section or foot. Drilling is accomplished on a lathe operating at slow speed (400 rpm). A lever-action ram-feed device is used to press the wood against the drill while a hand-held clamp is used to steady the billet during drilling. The barrel is drilled from both ends.

All the sections are then reamed with tapered shell reamers to bring the bore to final dimension. The mouthpiece reamer is not tapered except for the plug portion. Recorders are usually built with a uniform taper in the barrel bore but the Dolmetsch recorder barrel reamer is cut to produce a taper in three subtle stages of gradation. The jogs fall at nodal points that control octave spacing, Dr. Dolmetsch explains. The foot is reamed with a tapered

Recorder in F by Thos. Stanesby Sr., London
(d. 1734). Boxwood with ivory rings (Dolmetsch Collection).

*169. Drilling boxwood barrel with ram feed lever
and hand held clamp as steadying device*

170. *Preset gauge accurately marks barrel length*

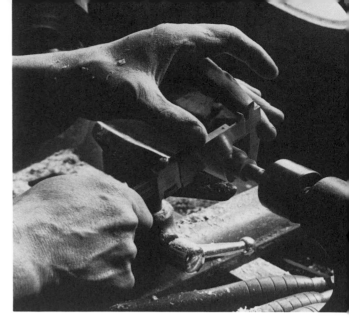

171. *Measuring barrel diameter*

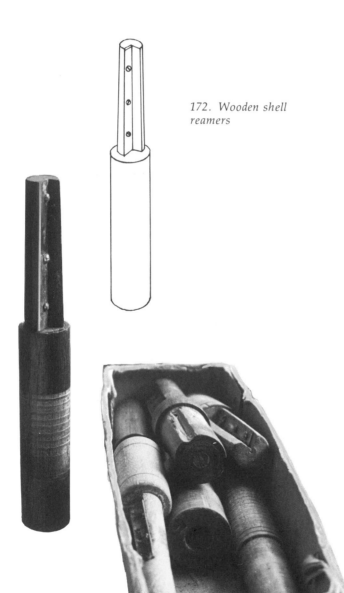

172. *Wooden shell reamers*

reamer that makes a smooth extension of the barrel bore through to the bell.

The reamed sections are then turned to cylindrical shape. Each section is mounted on a mandrel tapered to fit the bores, the face-plate end held rigid by a lathe dog. Each section is cut to exact length on the lathe. The size is marked off and turned down to a thin section, which is cut off with a sharp knife. The three sections are then reamed again to ensure that all have the correct bore.

A socket is bored in foot and mouthpiece with an end mill mounted in a drill press. The socket depth is gauged with great care as are the tenon ends of the barrel; the shoulders must butt tightly on both ends with the tenons seated against the bottom face of the sockets.

The barrel is remounted on its mandrel and turned down to finished dimension. The end tenons are channeled to receive the cork sleeve that will join the sections with a tight friction fit. A strip of cork sheeting is glued into the channel with a lap joint that is smoothed flush with sandpaper on the lathe. The mouthpiece and foot are turned to shape with the beading cut in mainly by eye. Smoothing is done on the lathe with garnet papers, beginning with #100 (coarse), ranging up to #240 (fine). Lathe speed for these turning operations is approximately 1300 to 1500 rpm.

A final run-through with the reamers to make

173. *Turning contour rings with diamond point tool*

174. *Fine sanding while work spins*

doubly sure that the bore is true completes this stage of construction. The joints are fitted together with a dab of lanolin on the cork to prevent seizing of the joint. A plug is inserted in the bell and the recorder is filled with banana oil, a trade name for an amyl acetate formulation of nitrocellulose lacquer. The plug is removed, the fluid drained, and the recorder hung up to dry. After an hour, the bore is cleaned with a rag pushed through with a dowel. This treatment leaves the bore glisteningly smooth and offers some protection against the moisture that occurs during playing.

Finger hole drills are kept in a color-coded box which also serves as a holding jig for positioning the drill holes. Drills are a mix of standard inch and metric sizes including numbered and letter drills. Thumb, second, and fifth holes are the same size. The double holes in the foot are drilled with a wedge under the box jig to give these holes their proper angle. A drilled ivory bushing is glued into the thumb hole, and the double hole fingering depressions are filed with a half-round file.

175. *Box jig for accurate drilling of finger holes*

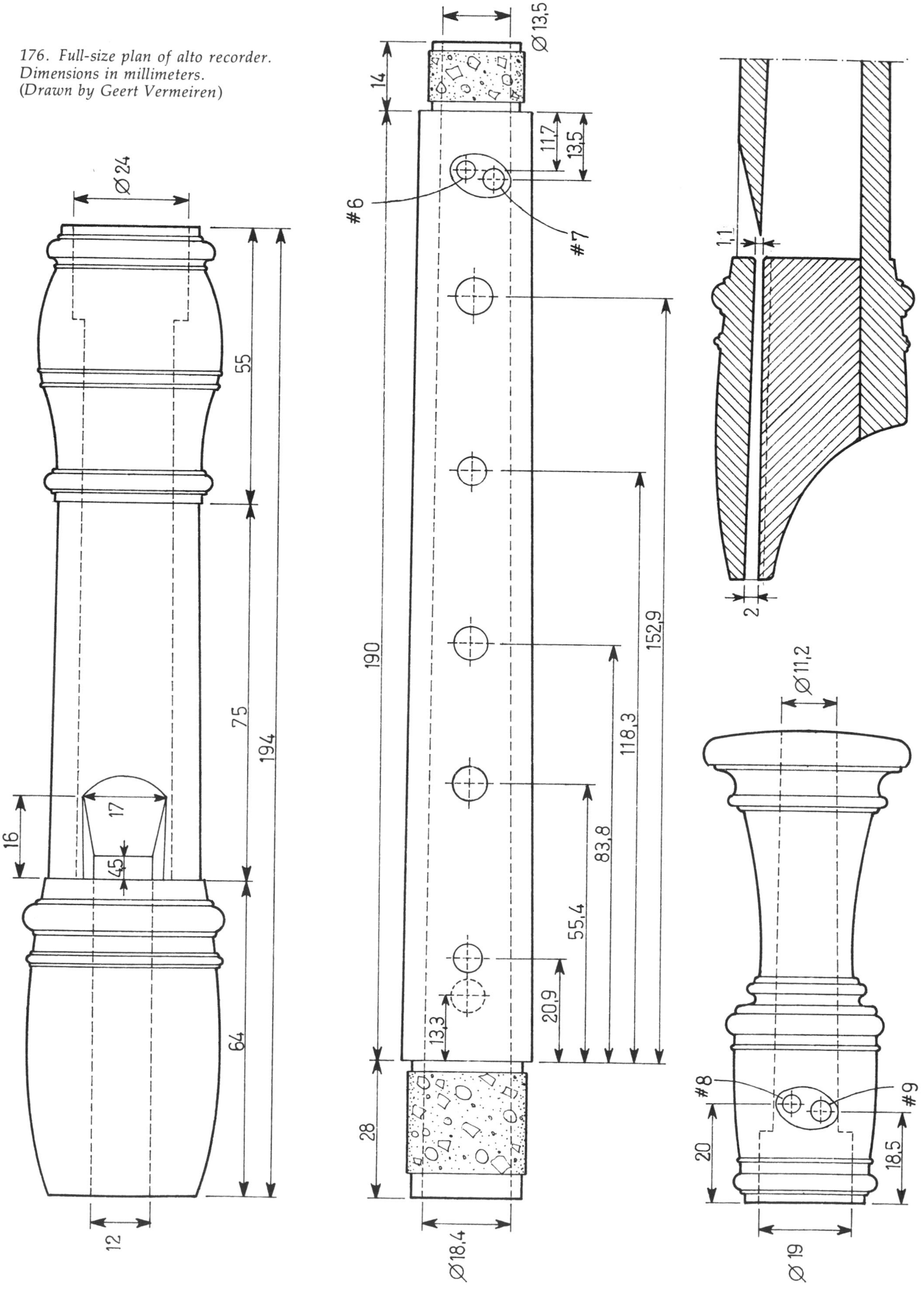

176. *Full-size plan of alto recorder.*
Dimensions in millimeters.
(Drawn by Geert Vermeiren)

Ø24

55

75

194

16

17

45

64

12

Ø13,5

14

117

13,5

#6

#7

190

152,9

118,3

83,8

55,4

20,9

13,3

28

Ø18,4

1,1

2

Ø11,2

#8

#9

20

18,5

Ø19

ALTO RECORDER FINGER HOLE SIZES

Hole	Drill	Dia. inches	Dia. millimeters
Thumb	I	.2720	6.9088
1.	#1	.2280	5.793
2.	I	.2720	6.9088
3.	H	.2660	6.7564
4.	7/32"	7/32	5.5562
5.	I	.2720	6.9088
6.	#29	.1360	3.454
7.	#22	.1570	3.988
*8.	#25	.1495	3.802
*9.	#21	.1590	4.039

*Note: Holes 8 and 9 drilled at 30 degree angle toward bell

177. Bandsawing mouthpiece held in box jig

Mouthpiece

Three small holes are drilled where the window gap falls, to facilitate knife and chisel entry. The side outline of the window is traced with a sharp knife and the ramp is cut at a shallow angle down to the drill holes. A chisel is used to cut down and define the sill end of the window and the gap is cleared out with a sharp knife. With the fipple edge (also wind cutter) at least 3/32" thick, the mouthpiece is fitted onto a lathe in a special spring-tensioned holding device with screw adjustment. A two-step broaching tool designed to cut both windway and slightly lower baffle is repeatedly pushed in and out of the mouthpiece with a lever-action ram-feed. Pressure is gradually increased on the mouthpiece, pressing it down onto the cutting edges of the broaching tool. A steadying support under the shank of the broaching tool helps ensure stability during this delicate operation. The windway is examined at frequent intervals while broaching proceeds. Rough cutting of the windway and baffle is followed by a finishing cut with a finer broaching tool.

Cutting of the underside of the mouthpiece is done on a bandsaw with the mouthpiece held securely in a box jig. The cutout is smoothed on a drum sander. Boxwood, because of its light color, soils easily and is sometimes covered with masking tape to keep it clean while it is being worked on.

The mouthpiece is mounted on a peg-shaped holding device secured in a vise to complete the cutting of the window and fipple edge. Chisel and knife are used to cut these to their final dimension. Cutting is done with slow precision to ensure that this critical area is flawlessly correct. Small, curved sanding sticks are used to smooth the ceiling of the windway and give it a slight degree of longitudinal arch. The underside of the fipple edge, the baffle, is also given a slight degree of longitudinal arch with a curved broaching tool inserted from the embouchure end. All of the windway surfaces are immaculately smoothed with fine garnet paper wrapped over small sticks.

The sides of the window are canted outward a few degrees and the fipple edge is finished to a

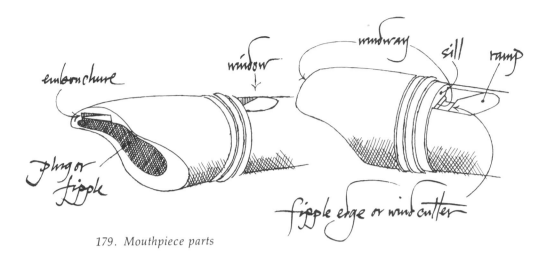

179. Mouthpiece parts

thickness between .010″ and .015″. A knife edge would quickly warp from moisture-laden air blown by the player. This edge cuts air blown through the windway about one-third of the windway height above the floor of the windway. The gap left between the end of the fipple plug and the fipple edge is about .175″ wide.

A red cedar plug turned to an oversize tapered shape is fitted to the mouthpiece in the final stage of construction. The long edges of the tongue are scribed with a sharp knife; chisel and bullnose plane define these edges. When the sides of the tongue are down about $5/64$″, the rounded top of the tongue is flattened with a block plane.

The plug is repeatedly tested for fit as tapering proceeds with block plane and file. A light wooden mallet taps the cedar plug in place so the fit can be examined under a strong light by sighting from both ends. The plug must make an airtight seal with the mouthpiece bore. The plug is knocked out with a light tap from the thin mallet handle. As tapering of the plug continually increases its interior access,

180. Cutting window with sharp knife

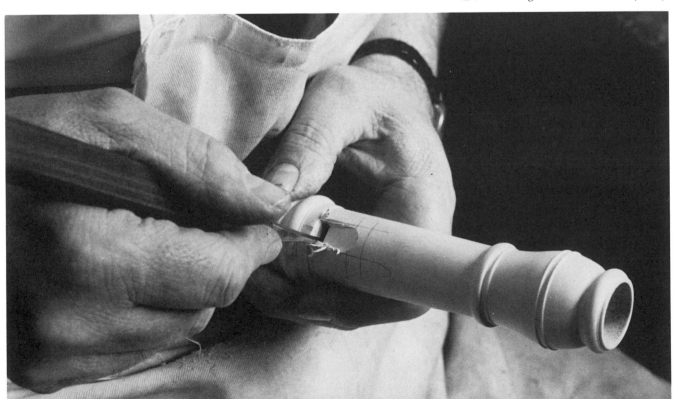

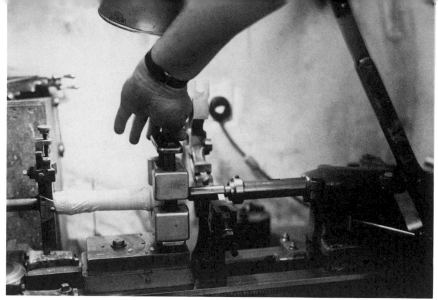

181. *Special broaching setup for cutting windway and baffle*
(two inch area extending forward from fipple edge toward barrel joint)

182. *Broaching tool*

183. *Fine sanding windway and baffle*

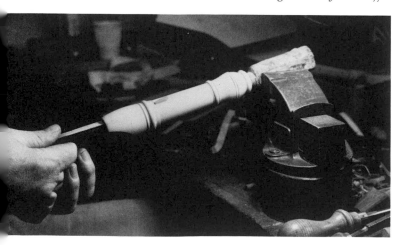

the sill end of the plug must be kept ground down to avoid striking and damaging the delicate fipple edge.

When the plug is finally seated with a moderate degree of forcing, the tongue is tapered from about $1/16''$ on the sill end to $3/64''$ on the embouchure end. The excess plug protruding from the mouthpiece is cut out with a chisel and sanded to a smooth continuity with the underside of the mouthpiece. Final sill end height of the windway is about .042″ and .085″ on the embouchure end. The last step in fitting the plug is to impart a slight concavity to the longitudinal face of the tongue—about .005″ at the center. The plug is held in place by friction, never glued.

At Arnold Dolmetsch Ltd. final voicing of each instrument is done personally by Dr. Dolmetsch and his close associates. Voicing techniques include subtle variations in finger hole size; flaring the underside of finger holes; slight modifications of windway; flaring of exit bore at bell; occasional rereaming of bore. The process begins by cutting slight chamfers in the sill end opening of the windway. As voicing proceeds, the instrument is played to test modifications and determine where further improvement is needed. Many instruments are voiced to specific requirements of expert players

*184. Dr. Dolmetsch flaring
inside edge of finger holes*

with well-defined ideas about the kind of tone they
want. This final, indispensable step in the construction of a recorder is one for which Dr. Dolmetsch
feels a personal responsibility. Each instrument re-
ceives the benefit of his unparalleled experience to
ensure that it will reach the player possessed of its
utmost capacity for a rich, balanced tone.

After voicing and tuning are completed, the recorder is hand-polished with a specially formulated
lacquer to enhance the grain and protect the wood.

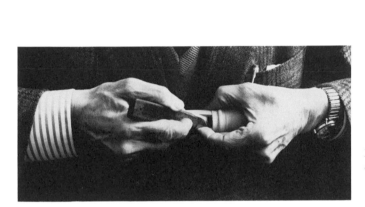

*185. Cutting small chamfers on sill
end of windway opening*

186. Final testing for pitch and tone quality

Bibliography

Baines, A. *European & American Musical Instruments*. New York: Viking, 1966.

Baines, A. *Musical Instruments Through the Ages*. Baltimore: Pelican Books, 1961.

Benade, A. H. *Horns, Strings and Harmony*. New York: Doubleday Anchor Books, 1960.

Blades, J. *Percussion Instruments and Their History*. London: Faber and Faber, 1970.

Buchner, A. *Musical Instruments Through the Ages*. London: Spring Books, 1961.

Campbell, M. *Dolmetsch: The Man and His Work*. London: Hamish Hamilton, 1975.

Cennini, C. *The Craftsman's Handbook*. New York: Dover, 1956.

Constantine, A., Jr. *Know Your Woods*. New York: Scribner's, 1959.

Gurvin, O. "The Harding Fiddle." *Studia Musicologica Norvegica 1*, Oslo, 1968. S. 14.

Hagberg, K. A. and Saporito, J. F. *"Early Developments in Tambourine Technique*, ca. 1800." Unpublished dissertation. Rochester, N.Y.: Eastman School of Music, 1975.

Heron-Allen, Ed. *Violin-Making as it was and is*. London: Ward Lock, 1885.

Hill, W. H. *Antonio Stradivari*. 1902. Reprint; New York: Dover, 1963.

Hines, C. *How to Make and Play the Dulcimore*. Harrisburg, Pa.: Stackpole Books, 1973.

Marcuse, S. *Musical Instruments, A Comprehensive Dictionary*. New York: Norton, 1975.

Mayer, R. *The Artist's Handbook of Materials and Techniques*. New York: Viking, 1950.

Montagu, J. *Making Early Percussion Instruments*. London: Oxford University Press, 1976.

Murphy, M. *The Appalachian Dulcimer Book*. St. Clairsville, Ohio: Folksay Press, 1976.

Osa, S. B. *The Hardanger Fiddle*. Oslo, Norway: Musikk-Huset A/S, 1952.

Robinson, T. *The Amateur Wind Instrument Maker*. Amherst, Mass.: University of Massachusetts Press, 1973.

Scruggs, E. *Earl Scruggs and the Five-String Banjo*. London: Music Sales, 1968.

Sevag, R. "The Harding Fiddle." In Mette Muller, ed., *From Bone Pipe and Cattle Horn to Fiddle and Psaltery*. Copenhagen: Musikhistorisk Museum, 1972.

Untracht, O. *Metal Techniques for Craftsmen*. New York: Doubleday, 1968.

Wake, H. S. *The Technique of Violin Making*. San Diego, Cal.: Published by the author, 1973.

Suppliers

A. Constantine & Son, Inc.
2050 Eastchester Rd., Bronx, New York 10461
Veneers, spring steel banding, precut discs for release forms, epoxy, woodworking supplies.

Metropolitan Music Co.
Mountain Road, R. D. #1, Stowe, Vermont 05672
Violin and dulcimer wood, tools, supplies.

Vitali Import Co.
5944 Atlantic Blvd., Maywood, California 90270
Violin and dulcimer wood, tools, supplies.

Woodcraft Supply Corp.
313 Montvale Ave., Woburn, Massachusetts 01801
Highest quality imported and domestic woodworking tools and supplies.

Brookstone Company
Peterborough, New Hampshire 03458
Silver solder, hard-to-find tools.

H. Behlen & Bro. Inc.
Box 698, Amsterdam, New York 12010
All wood finishing materials. (Minimum $20)

Stewart-MacDonald Mfg. Co., Inc.
P. O. Box 900, Athens, Ohio 45701
Banjo parts and accessories.

Liberty Banjo Company
2367 Main St., Bridgeport, Connecticut 06604
Banjo parts and accessories.

Bucks County Folk Music Shop
40 Sand Road, New Britain, Pennsylvania 18901
Banjo and instrument making supplies.

Henry Potter & Company
26-28 Grosvenor Road, Aldershot
Hants GU11 3DP, England
Military drums, drum accessories. (Ship worldwide)

Eames Drum Company
6 Drummer Lane, Wakefield, Massachusetts 01880
Drum making accessories.

Werco
2340 W. Nelson St., Chicago, Illinois 60618
Skin heads for drum, banjo, tambourine.

H. Band & Co., Ltd.
Brent Way, High Street, Brentford, Middlesex TW8 8ET
England
Cloudy-calf drum skins, white calf for banjo and tambourine only. (Ship worldwide)

Allcraft Tool & Supply Co.
215 Park Avenue, Hicksville, New York 11801
Metalworking tools and supplies.

Paul H. Gesswein & Co., Inc.
235 Park Avenue South, New York, New York 10003
Jeweler's and engraver's supplies. (Minimum $10)

John L. Rie div. Cresthill Industries Inc.
196 Ashburton Ave., Yonkers, New York 12010
Mother-of-pearl, abalone. (Minimum $20)

Conklin Brass & Copper Co., Inc.
322-324 W. 23rd Street, New York, New York 10011
Brass, nickel silver, phosphorus bronze, aluminum. (Minimum $15)

Vera's Art Box
752A Frederick Rd., Catonsville, Maryland 21228
Ivory saddles, nuts, odd-size pieces.

F. Friedlein & Co., Ltd.
718-20 Old Ford Rd., London E3 2TA
England.
Ivory.

Sydney Evans Ltd.
45 Regent Place, Birmingham B1 3NB
England
Woods, instrument making supplies.

Clifford Essex Music Co., Ltd.
20 Earlham St., London W.C.2
England
Banjo parts, accessories.

Scott E. Antes
905 North Avenue N.E.
Massillon, Ohio 44646
Expertly drawn full-size blueprints banjos, dulcimers, others.